BILLY BATSON
AND THE MAGIC OF
SHAZAM!

FAMILY
AFFAIR

BILLY BATSON AND THE MAGIC OF SHAZAM!: FAMILY AFFAIR

Published by DC Comics. Compilation and all new material
Copyright © 2020 DC Comics. All Rights Reserved. Originally
published in single magazine form in *Billy Batson and the Magic
of Shazam!* 1-12. Copyright © 2008, 2009, 2010 DC Comics.
All Rights Reserved. All characters, their distinctive likenesses,
and related elements featured in this publication are trademarks
of DC Comics. The stories, characters, and incidents featured in
this publication are entirely fictional. DC Comics does not read or
accept unsolicited submissions of ideas, stories, or artwork.
DC - a WarnerMedia Company.

DC Comics, 2900 West Alameda Ave.,
Burbank, CA 91505
Printed by LSC Communications,
Kendallville, IN, USA. 1/10/20.
First Printing.
ISBN: 978-1-77950-116-5

Library of Congress Cataloging-in-Publication Data is available.

PEFC Certified
This product is from
sustainably managed
forests and controlled
sources
PEFC/29-31-337   www.pefc.org

BILLY BATSON
AND THE MAGIC OF
SHAZAM!

FAMILY AFFAIR

MIKE KUNKEL
ART BALTAZAR
FRANCO
writers

MIKE KUNKEL
DAVID TANGUAY
colorists

MIKE KUNKEL
BYRON VAUGHNS
KEN BRANCH
STEPHEN DeSTEFANO
artists

STEVE WANDS
TRAVIS LANHAM
letterers

MIKE KUNKEL
collection cover artist

* THE MONSTER SOCIETY CODE

A	B	C	D	E	F	G	H	I	J	K	L	M	N	O	P	Q	R	S	T	U	V	W	X	Y	Z
Z	Y	X	W	V	U	T	S	R	Q	P	O	N	M	L	K	J	I	H	G	F	E	D	C	B	A

Use this decoder key to unlock the secret messages in this book!

I WOULD IMAGINE TO BE HARD TO BE THE NEW KID AT SCHOOL. THOUGH I NEVER HAD TO DEAL WITH THAT QUITE MYSELF. LIKE I SAID, I'M ANCIENT.

AND YET, I'M SURE IT CAN MAKE IT A LITTLE EASIER WHEN YOU YOURSELF CAN PRETEND TO BE YOUR OWN PARENT.

WHAT. ARE. YOU. DOING??

YOU KNOW, I HAVE NOOO IDEA HOW GROWNUPS PUT THESE THINGS ON.

WELLLL, SINCE THE SCHOOL YEAR HAS ALREADY STARTED, THEY WANT A PARENT MEETING TO WELCOME US TO THE SCHOOL.

UH HUH. BUT ARE YOU SURE ABOUT THIS? I MEAN, IT'S ONE THING WHEN YOU PRETENDED TO BE OUR "DAD" TO SIGN FOR THIS APARTMENT.

BRILLIANT, I MIGHT ADD.

ANYWAAAAY...

NOW YOU'RE GONNA GO TALK TO THE TEACHERS?

ACTUALLY IT'S THE PRINCIPAL. THE TEACHERS ARE BUSY TODAY SO I'M MEETING WITH A.... MS. AMELIA STRIKTA.

THE PRINCIPAL?!!

YEAH, AND SHE SOUNDS TOUGH. YOU BETTER NOT GET INTO ANY TROUBLE. I'D HATE TO HAVE TO MEET AND DISCUSS YOUR DETENTION.

ME GET IN TROUBLE?! HAH. LISTEN, DOOFUS, I'M NOT THE ONE WHO DOESN'T KNOW HOW TO DRESS LIKE A GROWNUP.

GOOOD LUCK.

WHAAAAAAT?

SO, "CAPTAIN MARVEL"...

...YOU ARE THE KID W-- NOW HAS -- MAGIC OF -- LIGHTNING

THE CRANE WAS SO EASY TO DISMANTLE AND DRAW YOU OUT INTO THE OPEN. YET, YOU DECIDE TO *SAVE* THESE PUNY WORMS WHEN YOU SHOULD *RULE* THEM.

BUT THAT'S OKAY.

FOR NOW I, *THEO ADAN--* KNOW WHO Y-- ARE. AND WHE-- *FINALLY* GET T-- MAGIC WORD-- FROM YOU...

...I'LL *SHOW* YOU HOW IT'S REALL-- *SUPPOSED* T-- BE USED.

MIKE KUNKEL: WORDS, PICS, HEART

STEVE WANDS: LETTERS **ADAM SCHLAGMAN**: ASSOC. EDITOR **JANN JONES**: EDITOR

SHADOWS.

THERE ARE SHADOWS EVERYWHERE IN THIS WORLD. IN HALLWAY CORNERS, DARK CAVES, OUR CLOSETS, EVEN UNDER OUR BEDS... AND SOMETIMES, IN THE HEARTS OF MEN.

SHADOWS CREEP AND SNEAK AND DUCK AND HIDE AWAY FROM LIGHT.

NOW THAT I HAVE GIVEN BILLY BATSON THE MAGIC OF MY NAME... SHAZAM, HE CAN TURN INTO CAPTAIN MARVEL. HE CAN BE A POWERFUL FORCE OF GOODNESS AND LIGHT.

BUT, UNFORTUNATELY, HE IS NOT THE ONLY ONE THAT GOT THE MAGIC OF MY NAME. THERE WAS ANOTHER.

AND CAPTAIN MARVEL NOW HAS TO DEAL WITH A SHADOW THAT I ACCIDENTALLY CREATED AGES AGO.

S H A Z A M !
SOLOMON — WISDOM
HERCULES — STRENGTH
ATLAS — STAMINA
ZEUS — POWER
ACHILLES — COURAGE
MERCURY — SPEED

ONE THAT REBELLED AGAINST THE LIGHT OF GOODNESS I OFFERED AND HELD ONTO DARKNESS.

I AM REMINDED IN A GOOD BOOK IT SAYS, "THERE ARE THOSE WHO REBEL AGAINST THE LIGHT, WHO DO NOT KNOW ITS WAYS OR STAY IN ITS PATHS."

THE REBELLIOUS SHADOW'S NAME IS THEO ADAM.

AND HE HAS COME BACK WITH HOPES TO USE MY MAGIC AGAIN TO TURN INTO HIS ALTER EGO... BLACK ADAM... AND BATTLE AGAINST ME WITH THE 7 DEADLY EVILS OF MAN.

HOWEVER, ADAM AND HIS EVILS STILL HAVE TO DEFEAT THE LIGHT OF CAPTAIN MARVEL. AND THAT IS NOT SO EASY...

FOR IN THAT SAME GOOD BOOK, IT ALSO SAYS, "HE SHOT ARROWS AND SCATTERED THE ENEMIES, BOLTS OF LIGHTNING AND ROUTED THEM."

MIKE KUNKEL: WORDS, PICS, HEART
STEVE WANDS: LETTERS
ADAM SCHLAGMAN: ASSOC. EDITOR
JANN JONES: EDITOR

BULLYING (V.)...THE ACT OF INTENTIONALLY CAUSING HARM TO OTHERS THROUGH VERBAL HARASSMENT, PHYSICAL ASSAULT, OR OTHER MORE SUBTLE METHODS OF COERCION SUCH AS MANIPULATION.

NOBODY LIKES BULLIES. **HOWEVER**, IT IS NOT PERMISSIBLE TO SIMPLY FEED THEM TO A 50-FOOT SEA SERPENT WITH ASCORBIC SALIVA... THOUGH WE ALL WISH WE COULD.

GREEE!

I SAY THE **BEST** THING TO DO IS TO FACE THEM. SHOW NO FEAR.

AND WITH THE MAGIC OF MY NAME... **SHAZAM.**

...YOUNG **BILLY BATSON** HAS BEEN GIVEN THE POWER TO TURN INTO **CAPTAIN MARVEL** AND FACE THE BULLIES OF THE WORLD.

Solomon = Wisdom!
Hercules = Strength!
Atlas = Stamina!
Zeus = Power!
Achilles = Courage!
Mercury = Speed!

HE NEEDS **ALL** THE MAGIC WORD'S POWER TO TAKE ON THE **7 DEADLY EVILS OF MAN** AND A BULLY NAMED **THEO ADAM**. ESPECIALLY WHEN THEO CAN TURN INTO AN EVEN BIGGER BULLY NAMED **BLACK ADAM**.

LUCKILY HE'S COME PREPARED FOR THE BULLIES. AS THE GOOD **DR. SEUSS** ONCE SAID, "I HAVE HEARD THERE ARE TROUBLES OF MORE THAN ONE KIND. SOME COME FROM AHEAD AND SOME COME FROM BEHIND. BUT I'VE BOUGHT A BIG BAT. I'M ALL READY, YOU SEE. NOW MY TROUBLES ARE GOING TO HAVE TROUBLES WITH ME!"

BECAUSE CAPTAIN MARVEL HAS LEARNED A SECRET ABOUT THE MAGIC OF SHAZAM. IT MAY GIVE POWER. BUT IF USED RIGHT...

...IT CAN ALSO TAKE THAT POWER AWAY.

selfishness
greed
pride
envy
laziness
injustice
hate

MIKE KUNKEL: WORDS, PICS, HEART
STEVE WANDS: LETTERS   **ADAM SCHLAGMAN:** ASSOC. EDITOR   **JANN JONES:** EDITOR

THERE YOU GO, GUYS! ALL *SAFE* AND *SOUND!*

AGAIN! AGAIN!

CAN YOU FLY ME TO CANADA?

NOW, REMEMBER TO DO YOUR HOMEWORK!

...BUT MY HOMEWORK'S STILL ON THE BUS!

CAN YOU GO BACK AND GET MY *TINY TITANS* LUNCHBOX?

SHAZAM!

KRA-KOOM

HEY! I WAS JUST WATCHING YOU ON TV. THAT MUST HAVE BEEN *SOME* FIELD TRIP!

YEAH! I'M GLAD I HAPPENED TO BE FLYING HOME THAT WAY!

WHERE ARE YOU GOING IN SUCH A HURRY?

I'M LATE FOR WORK. I NEED TO GET DOWN TO THE STUDIO AS *SOON* AS POSSIBLE. I HAVE SOME FOOTAGE OF CAPTAIN MARVEL I *NEED* TO GET TO MR. MORRIS.

HEY! THAT'S A SPIFFY SHIRT! WHAT'S THE OCCASION?

WELL, I JUST WANT TO LOOK GOOD FOR WORK, 'CAUSE WHEN YOU'RE A PROFESSIONAL JOURNALIST LIKE ME, YOU HAVE TO LOOK YOUR BEST.

OH BROTHER! THAT'S A BUNCH OF *HORSE HOCKEY!* IS THAT G-POD MESSING WITH YOUR BRAIN CELLS?

SPEAKING OF WHICH, DO YOU KNOW WHERE IT IS?

YEAH, RIGHT THERE ON THE TABLE WHERE YOU LEFT IT TWO SECONDS AGO.

OH, RIGHT! OKAY, SEE YOU!

BILLY? YOUR SHOES?

OH, RIGHT...

HAVE YOU GOT ANYTHING FOR *ME?*

I *SURE* DO! SOME *EXCLUSIVE* FOOTAGE OF *CAPTAIN MARVEL!*

THAT SCHOOL BUS THING? THAT'S BEEN ALL OVER THE NEWS!

UHHH...YEAH... THE SCHOOL BUS...THING.

IT'S BEEN RUN OF THE MILL LATELY WITH CAPTAIN MARVEL. THE STORIES ARE GOOD BUT THEY DON'T HAVE THAT SAME PUNCH AS WHEN THAT WHOLE THING WITH MR. MIND HAPPENED! IT'S NOT AS EXCITING!

HE'S *ALWAYS* EXCITING TO ME; I COULD WATCH HIM IN A BATHROBE EATING CORN FLAKES! ANY PLACE, ANYWHERE, ANY TIME...

MS. FIDELITY! COULD WE *FOCUS* HERE, PLEASE?

THAT WHOLE MR. MIND THING WAS RATINGS *GOLD!* NOW, *THAT* WAS A STORY! RATINGS WOULD SHOOT THROUGH THE ROOF IF SOMETHING BIG LIKE THAT WERE TO HAPPEN AGAIN...

"...BUT YOU NEVER KNOW WHEN A STORY LIKE THAT IS GOING TO BREAK!"

HEY DR. SIVANA, WHY HAVEN'T YOU DECORATED YOUR CELL YET? YOU SHOULD BE GETTING USED TO *PRISON* BY NOW.

YEAH! WHAT'S THE *MATTER?* NOT AS *GOOD* AS YOUR *CUSHY DIGS* WERE WHEN YOU WERE "ATTORNEY GENERAL OF THE UNITED STATES"?

BETTER GET USED TO IT; *YOU'LL* BE HERE FOR QUITE A AWHILE.

THAT'S WHAT YOU THINK!

DID YOU SAY SOMETHING, *CONVICT?*

OH, I MERELY SAID THAT I NEED A TISSUE TO WIPE MY GLASSES WITH... PLEASE.

TCK

BBZZZT

BBZZZT

BUT MR. MORRIS...SOMETHING LIKE THAT PUT HUNDREDS OF LIVES IN DANGER, ESPECIALLY CAPTAIN MARVEL'S LIFE.

LOOK MY BOY, IN THE NEWS BUSINESS, THE BEST STORIES ARE FILLED WITH BLOOD, SWEAT AND TEARS! BLOOD, SWEAT AND TEARS ARE RATINGS GOLD!

GOLD I TELL YOU!

BOOM

WWWWPRSSSSHHHHH!!!

CAN YOU SPELL BIG RATINGS WITH A *BIG GIANT ROBOT?*

BIG GIANT ROBOT ALSO MEANS CAPTAIN MARVEL WILL SHOW UP! *THERE'S* YOUR STORY, KID! *THERE'S* YOUR BLOOD, SWEAT AND TEARS RIGHT THERE!

SH—

BILLY! G-POD!

RIGHT, SIR!

DID HE JUST SHUSH ME?

SHOULDN'T YOU BE GOING, TOO?

OH! RIGHT YOU ARE, CHIEF!!

SHAZAM!

KRAK

SMACK

OKAY... THEY'RE JUST *COOL* TO LOOK AT! GETTING HIT BY ONE... *NOT* SO MUCH!

GGGGZZZHT

PHHSSSTTT

DON'T WORRY, *I'VE* GOT THIS COVERED!

MARY! *NO!*

WE DON'T KNOW IF YOU CAN SURVIVE SOMETHING LIKE THIS!

BOOM

BOOM

BOOM

SLAM

KABOOOF

RUMMMBLE

CRACK

OH MY GOSH!
OH MY GOSH!
OH MY GOSH!

ARE YOU OKAY?

LOOK OUT!!!

SLAM

THANKS.

YOU'RE MY HERO, CAPTAIN MARVEL!

UH... THANK YOU... CITIZEN.

THIS IS PROBABLY NOT GOING TO HELP BILLY AT ALL...

THE *WATER!!* WE NEED TO DRIVE HIM OUT INTO THE WATER SO HE CAN'T DO ANYMORE *DAMAGE* TO THE BUILDINGS OR HURT ANYONE!

ZIP

ZIP

ZIP

ZIP

ZIP

ZIP

CAPTAIN MARVEL! I'M DR. LANGLEY, I HAVE SOME *USEFUL* INFORMATION ABOUT MR. ATOM!

MR. WHO?

MR. *ATOM,* THE GIANT ROBOT!

YOU NAMED HIM?

PLEASE MAKE THIS *FAST* SO WE CAN DEAL WITH THIS WITHOUT *ANYONE* ELSE GETTING HURT.

I *CREATED* MR. ATOM! DR. SIVANA, THE *FORMER* ATTORNEY GENERAL, CLAIMED MR. ATOM IN THE NAME OF NATIONAL SECURITY, BUT WHAT HE REALLY DID WAS *STEAL* HIM!

HOW COULD SIVANA POSSIBLY DO *THAT?* HE'S SAFELY TUCKED AWAY IN JAIL!

SIVANA **CONFISCATED** MR. ATOM AS WELL AS PLANS FOR **SEVERAL** OTHER INVENTIONS OF MINE TO EVENTUALLY **SELL** AS WAR MACHINES, I FEAR! I'VE BEEN **TRYING** TO CUT THROUGH RED TAPE FOR YEARS, TRYING TO GET BACK ALL OF MY WORK.

SORRY TO INTERRUPT YOUR CONVERSATION...

...BUT I **COULD** USE A LITTLE HELP HERE!

WAIT! THERE'S A WAY TO **DEACTIVATE** HIM!

UUGH!

HANG ON!

I *REALLY* WISH HE HAD TOLD ME THAT *BEFORE* THIS WALKING JUNK PILE GOT ME IN A VISE GRIP!

IF SIVANA DIDN'T REDESIGN THE WHOLE THING, THERE SHOULD BE A *SWITCH* AT THE BASE OF MR. ATOM'S NECK!

GO! I CAN GET OUT OF THIS!

GOT IT!

CLICK

BZZZZT

SHAZAM!

KRA-BOOM

SHAZAM!

BOOM

OKAY, "MR. ATOM," YOU'RE TOAST!

NO!

KA-KRUNKH

HOOORAY!

I WAS SO WORRIED.

AS WAS I! I WAS *TRYING* TO TELL YOU THAT IF YOU BROKE THE ATOMIC POWER SUPPLY YOU WOULD CAUSE AN *EXPLOSION*... YOU WERE *SUPPOSED* TO TRY AND DISCONNECT IT.

SORRY I BROKE YOUR ROBOT, DOCTOR.

NOT TO WORRY, CAPTAIN, AS LONG AS *EVERYONE* IS SAFE, I CAN LIVE WITH THAT!

to be KING

Written By: Art Baltazar & Franco
Art By: Stephen DeStefano
Colors: David Tanguay
Cover: J. Bone
Asst. Editor: Simona Martore
Editors: Dan Didio & Rachel Gluckstern

GREETINGS, CAPTAIN MARVEL, MISS MARY. IT IS **GOOD** TO SEE BOTH OF YOU AGAIN.

MASTER, IS THERE SOMETHING WRONG? WHY HAVE YOU CALLED FOR US?

THE **STATUES,** MY BOY!

I DON'T SEE ANYTHING...

IT IS SLIGHT, BUT IT'S THERE. THE EYES ARE BEGINNING TO OPEN AND IT FEELS SOMEHOW... FAMILIAR AS WELL.

WELL, THEIR EYES ARE BARELY OPEN SO THE THREAT CAN'T BE THAT BAD! ...RIGHT?

AHHH BUT, YOUNG MISS THAT IS THE PROBLEM. IT MEANS THAT THERE IS SOMEONE OR SOMETHING **PLOTTING!**

PLANS ARE BEING PUT IN MOTION, AND I HAVE A FEELING THOSE PLANS ARE BEING PUT IN MOTION TO STOP OR HURT THE TWO OF YOU.

I'M NOT JUST TALKING ABOUT CAPTAIN MARVEL AND MARY MARVEL; I'M ALSO TALKING ABOUT BILLY AND MARY BATSON.

BUT WHO WOULD WANT TO HURT US? THE ONLY ONE WHO KNOWS THAT BILLY AND MARY ARE REALLY US IS DR. SIVANA, AND HE'S IN JAIL FOR A LONG, LONG TIME!

WHICH BEGS THE **QUESTION,** DEAR BOY, ARE YOU SURE HE IS STILL THERE?

WE DON'T KNOW HOW IT HAPPENED, CAPTAIN MARVEL. HE WAS *PROCESSED* BEFORE HE WAS BROUGHT HERE, WHICH MEANS HE WAS SEARCHED, BUT IT'S *OBVIOUS* HE USED SOMETHING TO CREATE THIS AND ESCAPE.

FIGURES... ONLY *SIVANA* IS *SMALL* ENOUGH TO FIT THROUGH THAT *HOLE.*

HE'S SMALL ALL RIGHT. THAT GUY'S A *WEASEL!* HE THREW ME OFF THE *MONSTER TOWER.*

WE NEED TO MAKE IT A *PRIORITY* TO FIND HIM! THANKS FOR YOUR TIME, WARDEN.

HEY THERE, TAWNY. YOU MIND IF WE SHARE SOME OF YOUR HEAT?

NOT AT ALL JOE! YOU KNOW YOU'RE WELCOME HERE *ANYTIME*. WHO'S YOUR NEW *FRIEND* THERE?

HE'S *NEW* AROUND HERE. I THOUGHT IT WOULD BE OKAY IF HE HUNG OUT WITH US A BIT. GEEZ, FELLA, I DIDN'T EVEN ASK YOUR *NAME*.

JUST CALL ME 'DOC,' FRIEND.

NICE TO MEET YOU, DOC.

SNAP CRACK

WHAT? WHAT IS *THAT*?

KIDS! RUN!!

I KNOW WE'RE ONTO THIS SIVANA STORY, BUT WHAT'S UP WITH THIS *BIGFOOT* SIGHTING IN THE MOUNTAINS?

IT'S A *JOKE!* DON'T BELIEVE IT!

WHY NOT?

I DON'T BUY IT... ALL THAT FOLKLORE MUMBO JUMBO MAGIC VOODOO STUFF. NEVER REALLY BOUGHT INTO ANY OF IT.

HOW DO YOU EXPLAIN *CAPTAIN MARVEL?*

UHM...

OR ALL THOSE *MONSTERS* FROM THAT *MR. MIND* FIASCO IN THE PARK A WHILE BACK?

OH YEAH...

THERE'S A MONSTER BACK THERE!

DON'T GO THERE!

THAT'S WEIRD.

I WONDER WHAT THAT'S ALL ABOUT.

LOOK OUT!!!

WHAT IS GOING ON?

THIS IS TOO *WEIRD.* THIS MAY HAVE SOMETHING TO DO WITH SIVANA--OR MAYBE *MR. MIND* IS BACK IF WE'RE DEALING WITH A MONSTER. I BETTER CHECK THIS OUT AS *CAPTAIN MARVEL.*

SHAZAM!

KA-
BOOOO

THIS MUST BE THE PLACE.

KRIIPPP

A CAVEMAN?

CAVEMAN?!! ENOUGH WITH THIS CAVEMAN! ALL OF THESE PUNY PEASANTS YELL CAVEMAN! MONSTER! BAH!

I AM NEITHER MONSTER NOR CAVEMAN! I WAS ONCE A RULER OF MEN! OF ALL MEN!

THIS TIME PERIOD HAS LIMITED INTELLIGENCE IF ALL THEY CAN SEE IS A CAVEMAN! I AM RULER OF ALL LIVING THINGS!

THOSE IN MY TIME CALLED ME BEASTMAN BECAUSE THEY FEAR ME! WITH GOOD REASON!

FOR I AM KING KULL!

...UH, OK... MR. ...KULL, I...

BAH! LEAVE, SO THAT I CAN FINISH THIS THRONE FROM WHICH TO RULE THIS WORLD!

IT'S NOT RUNNING SO I CALLED IN TO THE STUDIO. THEY'RE SENDING ANOTHER VAN OUT AS WE SPEAK.

GREAT! WHERE'S THE KID, THOUGH?

...HELLO.

UHM, HI.

OW...SO MUCH FOR *NOT* GETTING CAUGHT OFF-GUARD.

I DO NOT SUFFER *FOOLS GLADLY*--OR OTHERWISE!

I COME FROM A TIME LONG PAST AND WAS LEADER OF A BRUTISH BUT TECHNOLOGICALLY *ADVANCED* RACE!

THOOM

IT SEEMS IN THIS TIME PERIOD IT WILL BE AN EASY MATTER TO CONQUER! I WILL NOT MAKE THE SAME MISTAKES I MADE IN THE PAST.

I BECAME COMPLACENT THEN, AND WAS OVERTHROWN, BUT THAT WILL NOT HAPPEN NOW.

YOU MAY FIND WE ARE NOT MUCH DIFFERENT FROM PEOPLE IN YOUR TIME--

--WE BOTH *HATE* LOUDMOUTHS!

BAH! I DO NOT BELIEVE THAT!

IF THEY ALL FIGHT LIKE YOU, I SHOULD NOT HAVE A PROBLEM BECOMING SUPREME RULER OF ALL HERE!

SSWRUNCH

IF I'M GOING TO HAVE ANY CHANCE WITH THIS GUY, I'M GOING TO HAVE TO MOVE THIS FIGHT TO A LESS WOODED AREA.

YOU NEED TO LEARN QUICKLY, RED ONE!

YOU CANNOT DEFEAT ME! I WILL BE RULER HERE AS I HAVE BEEN IN THE PAST!

I BET I HAVE SOMETHING YOUR SUBJECTS IN THE PAST DIDN'T HAVE.

WHAT IS THAT?

THE SPEED OF MERCURY!

WHOOSH

BOOM

BUILDING COMPLEX UNDER DEMOLITION

FWOOM

NOT SO TALKY AND BRAGGY NOW, ARE YOU?

ERK!

YOU ARE WEAK, RED ONE! I HAVE DEFEATED MEN THAT THOUGHT THEY COULD STAND UP TO ME BEFORE!

YOU KEEP SAYING THAT...BUT I STILL DON'T KNOW WHERE OR WHEN YOU CAME FROM!

YOU FIGHT LIKE AN INEXPERIENCED *CHILD!* WHEN I GET MY HANDS ON YOU...

...I WILL SHOW YOU THAT I AM THE *WORLD'S MIGHTIEST WARRIOR!*

YEAH, WELL, LET ME INTRODUCE MYSELF--THEY CALL ME *CAPTAIN MARVEL, THE WORLD'S MIGHTIEST MORTAL!*

NOOOO!

SHADOWS. THIS IS A SUBJECT THAT UNFORTUNATELY BEARS REPEATING. THE PROBLEM WITH SHADOWS IS THEY ALWAYS COME BACK.

THE LIGHT CAN SHINE AND ILLUMINATE ONLY SO MUCH DARKNESS. WHEN THE LIGHT GOES AWAY, OR IS DIRECTED SOMEWHERE ELSE, THE SHADOWS COME BACK.

BILLY BATSON HAS THE MAGIC OF MY NAME... SHAZAM!

HE HAS THE ABILITY TO BECOME CAPTAIN MARVEL. HIS LIGHT HAS SPURNED MANY FROM THE SHADOWS.

HE HAS DEFEATED A SHADOW I ACCIDENTALLY CREATED AGES AGO, ONE THAT WAS NOT THE EMBODIMENT OF GOOD THAT I HAD HOPED FOR.

HE HAS DEFEATED A SHADOW THAT WAS CREATED BY ANOTHER, NOT INTENDED FOR EVIL, BUT STOLEN BY ANOTHER AND USED FOR THAT EXACT PURPOSE.

HE HAS HAD TO BATTLE A SHADOW FROM YEARS LONG PAST THAT CAME TO THE PRESENT THROUGH SUSPENSION OF TIME WHILE IN AN UNANIMATED STATE.

ONE SHADOW THAT HAS COME BACK AFTER SO LONG AND THAT I FEAR WILL DO SO AGAIN.

A RUTHLESS TYRANT OF A LEADER IN HIS TIME AND HE STROVE TO SPREAD HIS MALEVOLENCE IN THE HERE AND NOW.

HE HAS DEFEATED THESE FOES THAT CAME FROM SHADOWS AND EVIL, BUT THERE IS ONE EVIL THAT CASTS ONE OF THE BIGGEST SHADOWS. HE STILL LURKS IN THE DARK.

LURKING AND SEARCHING FOR THE RIGHT TIME TO EMERGE. HE HAS BLACKNESS THAT FILLS HIS HEART AND WANTS TO CAUSE PAIN FOR BILLY AND CAPTAIN MARVEL.

ONE CAN ONLY HOPE THE LIGHT IS STRONG ENOUGH TO DISPEL THE SHADOWS.

YOU... IT'S ALL BECAUSE OF YOU. YOU *RUINED* MY *LIFE!* AND IF IT'S THE LAST THING I EVER DO... I'LL GET MY REVENGE, YOU BIG RED CHEESE!

HEY *DOC!* HOW COME WE GOTTA SLEEP OUT HERE WHEN WE GOT A PERFECTLY GOOD WARM PLACE TO SLEEP?

NOT TO MENTION THE *OTHER* PLACE WE HAVE TOO.

YEAH! WE GOT *TWO PLACES* WE CAN STAY, YET WE'RE OUT HERE IN THE *COLD!*

I'VE *EXPLAINED* THIS TO YOU BEFORE. YOU--

EVENING JOE, BILL, DOC... HOW YOU BOYS BEEN? HAVEN'T SEEN YOU IN A WHILE. THOUGHT MAYBE SOMETHING HAD *HAPPENED* TO YOU.

ME AND A COUPLE OF THE OTHER GUYS WERE GOING TO COME LOOK FOR YOU TOMORROW.

OH! HEH HEH...NO NEED FOR THAT, YOU KNOW HOW THE *VAGRANT LIFE* CAN BE, WANDERING AIMLESSLY FROM PLACE TO PLACE...

HEH HEH. NO, NO TROUBLE HERE, JUST LIVING THE LIFESTYLE OF THE *BROKE* AND *HOMELESS...*

YES... WELL... GLAD TO SEE YOU BOYS ARE OK.

HAVE A *GOOD NIGHT!*

HOW MANY TIMES DO I HAVE TO *EXPLAIN* THIS? THAT IS *EXACTLY* WHY WE HAVE TO SLEEP OUT HERE. BECAUSE PEOPLE WILL WONDER WHERE WE'VE BEEN.

WE DO NOT WANT TO *ATTRACT* ANY *ATTENTION* TO THE WAREHOUSE OR THE BUILDING WHERE WE BROUGHT THAT *KULL STATUE.* EVERY ONCE IN A WHILE, FOR THE FORESEEABLE FUTURE, WE NEED TO PRETEND LIKE WE ARE STILL *HOMELESS,* SO SHUT UP AND GO TO SLEEP NOW!

THIS LOOKS LIKE SOMEONE TRYING TO HIDE SOMETHING AND DOESN'T WANT ANYONE ELSE TO KNOW WHAT IT IS.

WHAT IS *THIS?*

CURIOUSER AND CURIOUSER...

YES...YES I KNOW. I CHECK ON THEM EVERY ONCE IN A WHILE, FROM A *DISTANCE* OF COURSE.

THERE IS A *GREAT DANGER* LOOKING TO THREATEN BILLY AND MARY, IT HAS BEEN BUILDING FOR SOME TIME, BUT I FEAR IT WILL SOON COME TO PASS.

CAPTAIN MARVEL CAN TAKE CARE OF HIMSELF.

OF THAT I HAVE NO DOUBT, BUT I *FEAR* THE THREAT TARGETS HIS ALTER EGO, BILLY. AS *STRONG* AS THE BOY IS, THIS MAY BE SOMETHING THAT HE MAY NOT BE ABLE TO DEAL WITH.

THIS THREAT IS *DIFFERENT;* IT WILL STRIKE FROM WHERE WE DO NOT EXPECT IT TO STRIKE FROM, BUT I DO NOT KNOW *WHERE* THAT IS.

THIS *CAT* IS SOMEHOW INVOLVED WITH THE MARVELS! THIS IS A VERY *INTERESTING* TURN OF EVENTS!

I'LL GO BY IN THE MORNING AND CHECK ON THEM...

...IT MIGHT NOT BE A BAD IDEA TO CHECK ON THE *PEOPLE* AROUND THEM TOO, FRIENDS AND SUCH.

TAKE CARE AS YOU DO, TAWNY, FOR ONE CAN NOT SEE WHAT *HIDES* IN THE *DARK SHADOWS.*

YES, BY ALL MEANS... LEAD ME *DIRECTLY* TO THEM!

COME ON, BILLY! YOU'RE GOING TO MAKE US LATE... AGAIN!

I'M COMING! I'M COMING! DON'T GET YOUR LIGHTNING IN A TWIST!

IT AMAZES ME HOW MANY TIMES ONE PERSON CAN BE LATE TO THE SAME THING AT THE SAME TIME EVERY-DAY. THAT'S WHY THEY GIVE YOU A SCHEDULE AND CALL IT "SCHOOL!"

YEESH! WHAT DID YOU HAVE FOR CEREAL THIS MORNING, GROUCHY FLAKES?

THEY FIGURE THEY WOULD START IT THE SAME TIME EVERYDAY AND HOLD IT CONSECUTIVELY DAY AFTER DAY SO PEOPLE WOULD KNOW WHEN TO BE THERE.

I CAN'T HELP IT; I WAS UP LATE AS CAPTAIN MARVEL AGAIN.

WELL, THAT'S NO EXCUSE! YOU CHANGE INTO HIM AND GO FLYING OFF JUST TO AVOID DOING YOUR HOMEWORK.

NOW WAIT A MINUTE, YOU KNOW THAT'S NOT FAIR! THERE ARE LOTS OF PEOPLE OUT THERE THAT NEED CAPTAIN MARVEL'S HELP AND--

MARY? MARY, ARE YOU ALL RIGHT? WHAT IS IT?

TAWNY!!!

OH, TAWNY! I'VE MISSED YOU SO MUCH!

IT'S *GOOD* TO SEE YOU, TOO, *MARY.*

TAWNY!

WHERE HAVE YOU *BEEN?* WE HAVEN'T SEEN YOU IN SO LONG.

HELLO, BILLY.

I'VE BEEN *HERE* AND *THERE...* THOUGHT IT MIGHT BE TIME TO COME BY AND SEE HOW YOU TWO ARE DOING.

WAIT A MINUTE...WHAT'S *WRONG?*

WHAT ARE YOU TALKING ABOUT?

THE LAST TIME WE SAW YOU, WAS WHEN ALL OF THAT *MR. MIND* STUFF WAS HAPPENING AND THAT *LITTLE TROLL SIVANA* THREW ME FROM THE *MONSTER TOWER...*

THEN THAT WHOLE THING WITH *BLACK ADAM,* MR. ATOM AND EVEN *KING KULL...*

....AND YOU WERE NOWHERE TO BE SEEN.

WEEKS AND WEEKS HAVE GONE BY SINCE THEN AND NOW...

MARY!

...*OUT OF THE BLUE* YOU SHOW UP TO "JUST COME BY AND SEE HOW WE'RE DOING?" I DON'T BUY IT!

MARY! TAWNY I--

NO, BILLY, IT'S OKAY...SHE'S RIGHT. WE'RE **WORRIED**...

THE **WIZARD** IS WORRIED AS THE EYES ON THE STATUES HAVE NOW OPENED MORE AND THERE ARE **EVIL** THINGS HAPPENING. THE WIZARD IS CONVINCED THAT SOMETHING **BAD** IS GOING TO HAPPEN.

DOES IT HAVE SOMETHING TO DO WITH **SIVANA?**

WE'RE NOT SURE. MOST LIKELY HE WOULD BE THE **CULPRIT,** BUT WE CAN'T KNOW FOR CERTAIN.

WELL, YOU SHOULDN'T BE TOO WORRIED.

THERE'S NOTHING SIVANA CAN **THROW** AT US THAT CAPTAIN MARVEL CAN'T HANDLE.

AND MARY MARVEL TOO!

THAT MIGHT BE PART OF THE PROBLEM. THE **WIZARD** FEELS THAT THE THREAT MIGHT BE DIRECTLY AIMED AT THE **BOTH** OF YOU, BILLY AND MARY, AND NOT THE MARVELS.

LOOK. WE'VE BEEN ABLE TO **HANDLE EVERYTHING** THAT'S COME OUR WAY SO FAR. SIVANA IS NOTHING BUT A BUG HIDING UNDER A ROCK. AS SOON AS HE SHOWS HIS FACE, WE'LL HANDLE HIM **TOO!**

I'M SURE YOU'RE RIGHT... YOU CAN'T BLAME AN **OLD COOT** LIKE ME FROM BEING A BIT **WORRIED** ABOUT YOU YOUNGSTERS.

WOULD AN **OLD COOT** LIKE YOU MIND WALKING A COUPLE OF YOUNGSTERS TO SCHOOL?

NO, NOT AT ALL.

BECK & PARKER APARTMENTS

PERFECT! I'VE LOCATED THE *IP ADDRESS* OF THEIR COMPUTER AND ISOLATED IT.

WHY DO YOU HAVE SO MANY *WIRES* HOOKED UP TO THIS *STATUE?*

WHAT?

I'VE *TOLD* YOU BEFORE! I NEED TO BE ABLE TO MONITOR ALL OF HIS VITAL SIGNS AND BRAIN ACTIVITY.

WHY WOULD YOU WANNA DO *THAT?*

...LOOK AT HIM--HE'S A *STATUE!*

HE'S NOT A *STATUE!* HE'S STILL *ALIVE* ENCASED UNDER THAT METAL SHELL.

WITH THAT HEAD BAND I CREATED, I CAN PULL MEMORIES FROM HIS OCCIPITAL CORTEX AND *VIEW* THEM AS IF I'M WATCHING A TELEVISION PROGRAM!

...SO, WHY DO YOU HAVE HIM HOOKED UP TO ALL THESE WIRES?

NEVER MIND. JUST GET YOUR THINGS TOGETHER. WE HAVE *SOMEWHERE* TO BE.

JOE! STOP FOOLING AROUND WITH THOSE THINGS AND LET'S GET OUT OF HERE.

WE NEED TO GET TO THAT APARTMENT *BEFORE* THOSE KIDS GET BACK.

HMMMM. I DON'T KNOW IF I SHOULD GET THE *TUNA* OR THE *PB AND J*...HAVEN'T HAD THAT IN QUITE A WHILE. NOTHING LIKE A GOOD PB AND J WITH THE CRUST CUT OFF AND NICE COLD MILK.

WHAT DO YOU THINK?

ARE YOU TALKING TO *ME?*

YES. PB AND J OR TUNA?

HEY, DON'T I KNOW YOU? YOU'RE BILLY'S FRIEND... *TAWNY*, RIGHT?

TAWKY TAWNY. THAT'S ME.

I HAVEN'T SEEN YOU SINCE THE PARK, AND THAT WAS QUITE SOME TIME AGO.

OH. THANK YOU.

THAT WHOLE BUSINESS IN THE PARK HAD ME QUITE UNSETTLED FOR A TIME, BUT THAT BILLY SURE WAS A *BRAVE LITTLE FELLOW.* I HEAR TELL HE'S WORKING WITH YOU AT THE STUDIO NOW.

YES, HE'S OUR GO-TO GUY WITH ALL THINGS *CAPTAIN MARVEL.*

SO, HE'S DOING A FINE JOB THEN, IS HE?

OH, YES. IF I CAN FIGURE OUT HOW HE GETS ALL THOSE *EXCLUSIVES* ON CAPTAIN MARVEL, I MIGHT JUST EARN MY OWN REPORTERS BADGE.

BUT I THOUGHT YOU ALREADY WERE A *REPORT--*OH, I SEE! YOU'RE PULLING MY LEG!

YES, THAT'S WHAT I DO: *REPORTER SLASH COMEDIENNE.* WHAT BRINGS YOU TO THIS PART OF TOWN?

I HEAR THEY'VE GOT THE BEST PEANUT BUTTER AND JELLY SANDWICHES... AND TO ASK ABOUT BILLY AND SEE HOW HE'S DOING. THAT BOY'S PRACTICALLY BECOME LIKE *FAMILY.*

YEAH, HE'S A *GOOD* KID.

...AND YOU HAVEN'T SEEN HIM BEING BOTHERED OR FOLLOWED BY ANYONE LATELY?

WELL, THAT'S KIND OF A *STRANGE* QUESTION. IS THERE SOMETHING WE SHOULD BE *CONCERNED* ABOUT WITH BILLY?

OH NO. IT'S JUST AN *OLD DODDERING FOOL* LIKE ME SHOWING CONCERN FOR THE BOY. YOU HAVE A JOB THAT HAS YOU FOLLOWING AROUND CAPTAIN MARVEL, YOU'RE BOUND TO RUN INTO ONE OF HIS *ENEMIES* ONCE IN A WHILE.

I GUESS YOU'RE RIGHT. NO NEED TO BE CONCERNED, HE'S JUST *FINE.* LISTEN, THANKS FOR THE PB AND J.

I NEED TO GET BACK TO *WORK.* MAYBE WE'LL RUN INTO EACH OTHER AGAIN SOMETIME.

AAAAIEEE!

THUMP

WHAT WAS THAT DOC?

AN *UNFORESEEN EVENT* BUT STILL THE SAME RESULT! HE IS *UNCONSCIOUS.*

YOU'RE NOT KIDDING! HE *WENT OUT* LIKE A LIGHT!

WHAT DID YOU *DO* TO *HIM?*

IT WAS THIS *WHISTLE.*

WHISTLE? I DIDN'T *HEAR* A THING!

OF COURSE YOU DIDN'T. IT'S LIKE A DOG WHISTLE BUT EMITS A *FREQUENCY* ONLY FELINES CAN HEAR. I PULLED THE IDEA FROM *KING KULL'S BRAIN.*

NOW, *QUICKLY!* LET'S GET HIM OUT OF HERE!

WE SHOULD BE STARTING OUR **HOMEWORK** BEFORE IT GETS TOO LATE.

CAN WE WAIT UNTIL NORTH AMERICA'S MOST WANTED HUMOROUS DVD IS OVER?

HELLO THERE, **BATSONS!** SO NICE TO FIND YOU AT **HOME** THIS FINE EVENING!

WHAT THE--?

BILLY! LOOK! THE COMPUTER!

SIVANA!

SURPRISED TO SEE ME YOU **LITTLE BRATS?**

WHO YOU CALLING LITTLE? FROM WHAT I REMEMBER YOU'RE PRETTY **VERTICALLY CHALLENGED** YOURSELF!

AH YES, HOW I'VE **MISSED** THAT SHARP, POINTED HUMOR.

NEVER MIND THAT! HOW DID YOU GET IN THERE? WHERE ARE YOU?

WHEN I WAS WORKING WITH THE GOVERNMENT, WE DEVELOPED A **COMPUTER VIRUS** TO HACK INDIVIDUAL COMPUTERS. I APPROPRIATED IT BEFORE WE PARTED. OF COURSE THIS WAS MADE EVEN EASIER TO **ISOLATE** YOUR COMPUTER ONCE I LEARNED WHERE YOU LIVE.

HE KNOWS WHERE WE LIVE?

YES. **YES I DO!** AND YOU TWO LOOK VERY SCARED THERE STANDING IN FRONT OF YOUR COMPUTER! OH, BY THE WAY, YOU LEFT THE LIGHT ON IN THE OTHER ROOM.

HE'S **WATCHING US** FROM CLOSE BY!

SHAZAM!

YES, DO FOLLOW *MARVELS*, AS IT WILL LEAD YOU *DIRECTLY* TO ME!!!

COME TO ME, SO THAT I CAN *PAY YOU BACK* FOR ALL YOU HAVE DONE TO ME! IT'S TIME I TAKE MY *REVENGE* ON THE MARVEL FAMILY!!!

IT'S ALL ABOUT YOU, ISN'T IT? YOU DON'T CARE ABOUT WHAT YOU'VE DONE! YOU *HURT* PEOPLE AND YOU DON'T CARE!

ALL I KNOW IS THAT YOU ARE GOING *DOWN!* SO WE'RE GOING TO STOP YOU AND PUT YOU IN *JAIL* FOR A LONG, LONG TIME!

WHEN ARE YOU GOING TO LEARN, YOU *BIG RED CHEESE?* THERE IS NO PRISON OR PERSON THAT CAN EVER CONTAIN THE *POWER* AND *INTELLECT* OF DR. SIVANA!

MORE LIKE *DR. QUACK!* BECAUSE YOU'RE CRAZY YOU *NASTY OLD MAN!*

WHO'S *CRAZY* NOW, *LITTLE GIRL?* THE BRILLIANT SCIENTIST IN A MACHINE THAT HAS JUST *OVERPOWERED* YOU OR THE BIG RED CHEESE AND HIS MINI BABYBEL SIDEKICK?

WHAT IS IT WITH YOU? DO YOU HAVE THIS TYPE OF *OBSESSION* WITH DELI MEATS TOO OR JUST CHEESE?

MAKE ALL THE *JOKES* YOU WANT, YOU LITTLE BRAT, BUT THE TRUTH IS *YOU'RE IN TROUBLE!*

ENOUGH!!!

KLANK

I GUESS THAT SHOWED HIM.

YEAH...BUT *WHERE* IS HE?

STILL *ALIVE* AND *KICKING*...

AND ABLE TO *FIGHT* ANOTHER DAY!

YOU'RE NOT GETTING AWAY THAT EASY, SIVANA!

DO YOU REALLY THINK I WANT TO GET AWAY?

WHAT YOU DON'T REALIZE IS THAT I'VE *INVESTED* QUITE A CONSIDERABLE AMOUNT OF *TIME* INTO PUTTING MY PLAN TOGETHER!

WHAT *PLAN* IS THAT?

OH...*JUST THIS!*

SKROOM SKROOM

WHEN I ACTIVATED **MR. ATOM,** I WAS LOOKING FOR A DISTRACTION TO TAKE THE EYES OF **FAWCETT CITY** AWAY FROM THE PENITENTIARY I WAS IN, SO I COULD MAKE MY **ESCAPE.**

THANKS TO YOU, "BILLY," FOR **FIGHTING** HIM IN FRONT OF ALL THOSE CAMERAS.

...BUT YOU SEEMED TO HAVE A BIT OF A **TOUGH TIME** WITH HIM.

DON'T WORRY! I'LL DO THE SAME THING TO THIS ONE!

WE WILL!

AH AH AH! THIS ONE IS GOING TO BE REALLY **TOUGH** TO **DEFEAT.** YES, HE'S BIGGER AND I THINK YOU WOULD EVENTUALLY FIND A WAY TO **DESTROY** IT, TOO...

...BUT I'VE TAKEN **PRECAUTIONS** TO ENSURE THAT WON'T HAPPEN!

TEK

YOU SEE, THIS TIME I'VE *INSTALLED* MY CONTROL ROOM DIRECTLY INTO THE *ROBOT*, NOT A REMOTE LOCATION AS I HAD DONE WITH *MR. ATOM*, THUS MAKING ME THE BRAIN!

HHHHMMMM

THE LIGHTNING I *STOLE* FROM YOU GIVES THE ROBOT THE *LIFE FLOW*, THUS MAKING IT THE SOUL OF THE ROBOT.

HHHHMMMM

BUT I EVEN WENT A *STEP FURTHER* TO *INSURE* MY REVENGE!

EVERY ONE KNOWS THAT A GIANT TIN MAN LIKE THIS NEEDS A *HEART*...

TAWNY!!!

OH NO...

....AND I FOUND ONE!!!

DECEPTION RECEPTION

WRITTEN BY: ART BALTAZAR & FRANCO
ART BY: BYRON VAUGHNS
COLORS: DAVID TANGUAY LETTERS: SWANDS
COVER: BYRON VAUGHNS
ASST. EDITOR: SIMONA MARTORE
EDITOR: DAN DIDIO

TECHNOLOGY.

IT SEEMS THE WORLD RELIES UPON TECHNOLOGY MORE AND MORE AS TIME GOES BY. WHEN PEOPLE PUT MORE **FAITH** IN THINGS LIKE TECHNOLOGY, FAITH IN OTHER THINGS SEEMS TO FADE.

I FIND THAT PEOPLE TODAY DO NOT BELIEVE IN **MAGIC** AS MUCH AS THEY USED TO. EVERYONE PUTS FAITH IN THINGS THAT ARE TANGIBLE.

TECHNOLOGY IS SOMETHING THAT IS TACTILE- THE RESULTS ARE THERE FOR YOU TO SEE IMMEDIATELY.

CAPTAIN MARVEL AND LITTLE MARY MARVEL SEEM TO BE IN A **DILEMMA**, CAUGHT IN THE GRIP OF A GIANT TECHNOLOGICAL MONSTER POWERED BY THE ENERGY OF MAGIC CREATED BY ANOTHER MONSTER! DR. SIVANA!

HE IS AN EVIL BEING BENT ON DESTRUCTION OF THE MARVELS. HE HAS FOUND A WAY TO MIX TECHNOLOGY AND MAGIC TO DO HIS BLACK, TWISTED BIDDING.

HE HAS **CORRUPTED** THE TECHNOLOGY OF DR. LANGLEY, AND TECHNOLOGY FROM A BYGONE ERA DEVELOPED BY KING KULL AND INFUSED IT WITH MY OWN MAGICAL LIGHTNING!

TO ENSURE VICTORY, SIVANA EVEN WENT TO GREAT LENGTHS TO CAPTURE TAWKY TAWNY.

TAWNY'S LIFE FORCE IS SLOWLY EBBING AWAY AS IT IS USED BY SIVANA'S MECHANICAL MONSTROSITY TO DEFEAT CAPTAIN MARVEL.

I WONDER IF THE POWER OF **SHAZAM** IS ENOUGH TO DEFEAT SIVANA AND HIS EVIL PLANS...I CAN ONLY HOPE AND HAVE FAITH THAT IT DOES...

SOLOMON...WISDOM
HERCULES...STRENGTH
ATLAS...STAMINA
ZEUS...POWER
ACHILLES...COURAGE
MERCURY...SPEED

NOW THAT THIS ROBOT IS BEING *POWERED* BY THE MAGIC OF YOUR FRIEND TAWKY TAWNY AND YOUR OWN LIGHTNING, IT WILL BE LIGHTS OUT FOR THE MARVEL FAMILY!!

NOT SO FAST, SIVANA! WE DEFEATED MR. ATOM LAST TIME--

ARRRGHH!!

TAWNY!!!

YOU LET TAWNY GO, YOU NASTY LITTLE TROLL!!

MARY!!!

OW! THAT HURT!

KAKLANG

I'VE BEEN WORKING TOWARDS THIS MOMENT EVER SINCE YOU MARVELS THWARTED MY ATTEMPT TO CAPTURE THE POWER OF *MR. MIND* AND HIS *MONSTER SOCIETY.*

OH, I ADMIT THAT I NEEDED TO GET A BIT LUCKY AND HAVE A FEW THINGS FALL INTO PLACE IN ORDER TO EXACT MY *REVENGE,* YET HERE WE ALL ARE! ALL THINGS COME TO THOSE WHO WAIT!

MR. ATOM MIGHT HAVE BEEN JUST A DISTRACTION SO I COULD BREAK OUT OF JAIL, BUT THEN I KNEW I HAD THIS BIGGER ROBOT WAITING!

STEALING THE TECHNOLOGY TIDBITS FROM THE MIND OF THAT BRUTISH BARBARIAN KING KULL HELPED ME BRING THIS ROBOT UP TO SPEED AND WORKING ORDER, BUT THE TRUE POWER CAME FROM YOU, MARVELS!

THIS ROBOT HAS LIGHTNING IN ITS VEINS, ALL PUN INTENDED, THAT JUST MAKES HIM SO POWERFUL! THE THING THAT PUTS IT AND SIVANA OVER THE TOP, YOU ASK? YOUR FRIEND TAWNY!

THAT CAT'S MAGIC IS PURE ENERGY!

ALL OF THESE THINGS CAME TOGETHER JUST SO I CAN END THE *THREAT* OF CAPTAIN MARVEL AND SAVE THE AMERICAN PEOPLE!

MAWOOWOOO

ARRRGGH!!

FOR INSTANCE: THIS LITTLE BIT OF INSPIRED TECHNOLOGY THAT I PULLED FROM KULL'S OAFISH BRAIN...!

I PUT A MODERN *TWIST* ON IT. I TOOK HIS IDEA AND ADDED MICROWAVES AS A DELIVERY METHOD THAT DIRECTLY STRIKES THE NERVOUS SYSTEM AND VOILÀ...INSTANT PAIN.

ARRRGGH!!

MAWOO

I SIMPLY CALL IT *"THE PAIN BEAM."*

AIIIEE!!

WHAT?

YOU HAVE DONE *THIS* TO ME!

KULL? BUT HOW DID YOU--?

YOU WILL PAY *DEARLY* FOR THIS!

IF YOU ASK ME, IT LOOKS LIKE AN IMPROVEMENT.

DON'T YOU KNOW WHEN TO KEEP YOUR *TRAP* SHUT?

WHAT'S THE--

OH BOY! THIS COULD NOT BE GOING ANY BETTER!

KULL DOESN'T CARE ABOUT ME AT ALL. THE ONLY THING HE IS INTERESTED IN IS *BEATING* THE SNOT OUT OF THAT BIG RED CHEESE!

THE TRUCK!

BAH! YOU ARE FOOLS!!

WHAT FORM OF SORCERY IS THIS?

WHAT IS HAPPENING?

IF YOU ACTUALLY WENT TO SCHOOL MORE OFTEN AND PAID ATTENTION TO SOME OF THE CLASSES, SAY, FOR INSTANCE, SCIENCE CLASS, YOU WOULD LEARN THAT WHAT I JUST DID WAS JUST MAKE HIS ARM A GIANT MAGNET.

HIS ARM IS MADE OF METAL, SO I WRAPPED A COPPER WIRE AROUND IT AND ELECTRIFIED IT WITH A HUGE AMOUNT OF ENERGY...MAKING IT A MAGNET!

A VERY STRONG MAGNET!

I FEEL LIKE I SHOULD LEND A HAND!

BY ALL MEANS.

WRENCH

WELL DONE, MY YOUNG CHARGES.

YOU CONTINUE TO PROVE YOURSELVES WITH TENACITY, WISDOM AND COURAGE.

...BUT I FEAR THE FIGHT IS *FAR* FROM OVER!

COME TOGETHER!

RITTEN BY: ART BALTAZAR & FRANCO   ART BY: BYRON VAUGHNS
OLORS: DAVID TANGUAY   LETTERS: TRAVIS LANHAM
VER: BYRON VAUGHNS   ASST. EDITOR: SIMONA MARTORE   EDITOR: DAN DIDIO

FIRE FIRE EVERYWHERE!

WRITER: ART BALTAZAR & FRANCO   ARTIST: BRYON VAUGHNS   COLORS: DAVID TANGUAY   COVER: BRYON VAUGHNS
LETTERS: TRAVIS LANHAM   ASST. EDITOR: SIMONA MARTORE   EDITOR: DAN DIDIO

GLOWING EMBERS BURN DEEP IN THE RECESSES OF DARKNESS.

A FIRE MAY SEEM LIKE IT IS NO LONGER BURNING, BUT SOMETIMES DEEP IN THE COALS THERE ARE EMBERS.

THE FIRES **SEEM** TO HAVE BEEN PUT OUT. THINGS **SEEM** TO HAVE CALMED DOWN AND RETURNED TO NORMAL. CAPTAIN MARVEL AND MARY MARVEL HAVE SEEMINGLY PUT AN END TO THE THREAT THAT IS **DR. SIVANA** AND THE INTELLECTUAL BARBARIAN **KING KULL**.

THE HEROIC DUO HAS RESCUED TALKY TAWNY FROM THE PRECIPICE OF **DEATH** WHILE HE WAS IN THE HANDS OF SIVANA AND USED AS A PAWN TO **STRIKE** AT THE HEART OF MAGIC.

HAVING NEARLY TOPPLED THE BRAVE CAPTAIN AND HIS STEADFAST YOUNGER SIBLING, SIVANA MANAGED TO **ESCAPE** AND HAS NOT BEEN SEEN SINCE.

TAWNY, ALTHOUGH STILL WEAK FROM HIS ORDEAL, NOW RESTS **COMFORTABLY** IN THE HOME OF BILLY AND MARY BATSON.

THERE ARE **DANGERS**, HOWEVER, THAT **STILL** REMAIN AND ARE NOT VISIBLE TO ME AT THE MOMENT.

THE EYES OF THE STATUES OF THE 7 EVILS ARE OPEN...**SLIGHTLY**. TO THE **UNTRAINED EYE**, THEY WOULD SEEM AS IF NOT OPEN AT ALL, BUT THEY ARE.

IT MEANS THAT THERE IS EVIL LURKING ABOUT, IN THE SHADOWS AND THE DARKNESS.

IT IS AN EVIL **DEEP** UNDERCOVER THAT WILL ONLY EMERGE WHEN IT IS READY TO REVEAL ITSELF. LIKE A GLOWING EMBER...

...IF THE FIRE IS NOT PROPERLY PUT OUT, THOSE SAME GLOWING EMBERS CAN COME **ROARING** BACK INTO A **RAGING** CONFLAGRATION THAT NO ONE CAN EXTINGUISH.

THERE IS THIS FEELING OF FOREBODING THAT IS **GROWING** AND THAT I CAN NOT ESCAPE...

THANK YOU CAPTAIN MARVEL, THANK YOU!

≈COUGH COUGH≈

HEY! WHY DIDN'T YOU WAIT FOR ME?

WELL, YOU KNOW... *PEOPLE* TO SAVE, *FIRES* TO PUT OUT.

THERE'S NO TIME TO WAIT FOR SLOW-POKES.

I ONLY TOOK A *MINUTE* LONGER, AND I'M MUCH *FASTER* THAN YOU ARE ANYWAY...

... BUT I WAS JUST TELLING *TAWNY* WE WERE COMING TO THE FIRE SO HE WOULDN'T *WORRY* IF HE DIDN'T FIND US IN THE APARTMENT WHEN HE WOKE UP.

CLAP

WHOOSH

CAPTAIN MARVEL.

THANK YOU FOR HELPING OUT, IT WOULD HAVE TAKEN *HOURS* FOR US TO PUT THAT OUT.

THERE'S BEEN A RASH OF THESE LATELY THAT HAVE BEEN *DELIBERATELY* SET AND WE SURE ARE KEEN TO *CATCHING* THIS *DIRT BAG* AND PUTTING AN *END* TO THESE FIRES.

IT WOULD BE GREAT IF *YOU* COULD HELP CATCH THIS... *WHOEVER* IT IS!

CAPTAIN MARVEL?

CAN WE HAVE A WORD WITH YOU?

EXCUSE ME...

...COULD I HAVE A *HOT DOG* WITH ONIONS *AND* MUSTARD?

WELCOME BACK--

HEY TAWNY, **NO TIME** FOR SMALL TALK. GOING TO GRAB A DRINK AND THEN HIT THE **SACK.** SEE YOU IN THE MORNING.

SHAZAM!

KRA-KOOM

HELLO TAWNY, HOW ARE YOU **FEELING?**

OH, HELLO MARY. BACK SO SOON?

NO WORRIES WHEN YOU'VE GOT THE **BIG GUY** ON THE JOB.

YES, WELL, I SUPPOSE SO...

IS EVERYTHING ALL RIGHT, TAWNY? ARE YOU **COMFORTABLE?** ARE YOU IN **PAIN?**

OH NO, MARY, **EVERYTHING** IN THAT REGARD IS FINE. I'M FEELING STRONGER AND STRONGER EVERY DAY! I THANK YOU AND BILLY SO MUCH FOR LETTING ME RECUPERATE HERE IN YOUR APARTMENT.

I MUST ADMIT THAT I AM VERY COMFORTABLE ON THE STREETS BUT OLD BONES LIKE MINE CAN **DEFINITELY** GET USED TO THIS...

IT'S **BILLY** I'M **CONCERNED** ABOUT.

APPARENTLY THE ONLY THING **BILLY** IS **CONCERNED** ABOUT IS **BILLY.**

YES, I'VE NOTICED HE'S BECOME A BIT MORE **RECLUSIVE,** STAYING TO HIMSELF A LOT MORE. IS EVERYTHING ALL RIGHT WITH HIM?

OH, DON'T WORRY ABOUT HIM. YOU JUST CONCENTRATE ON GETTING **YOURSELF** ALL BETTER. BILLY WILL BE FINE...

...I HOPE.

YEAH, SO?

Y'KNOW, NOW THAT I *THINK* ABOUT IT...I DON'T THINK YOU'VE CHANGED INTO BILLY FOR A *FEW DAYS* NOW.

AGAIN... YEAH, SO?

...AND YOU DON'T FIND THIS *STRANGE?*

WHAT I FIND *STRANGE* IS YOU. NOW WHY DID *YOU* COME IN HERE?

OH MY *GOSH!* I *COMPLETELY* FORGOT! THERE'S ANOTHER FIRE!

WHAT? HOLY MOLEY, MARY!!! DON'T YOU THINK *THAT'S* IMPORTANT ENOUGH TO MENTION *FIRST?*

HELLO, CAPTAIN MARVEL.

CHIEF, ANY CLUES THIS TIME?

ACTUALLY, WE MAY HAVE GOTTEN *LUCKY* IN MORE WAYS THAN ONE HERE, CAP! THE BUILDING WAS ABANDONED AND WE HAD A *WITNESS* THIS TIME.

HE SAYS THAT SHE SAW A GUY RUNNING OFF BEFORE ANY EMERGENCY PERSONNEL ARRIVED ON SCENE. SHE'S BEING INTERVIEWED BY THE POLICE RIGHT NOW.

HE WAS WEARING A SKI MASK AND IT LOOKED LIKE A...SCUBA TANK ON HIS BACK.

A *SCUBA TANK?*

UHM... I KNOW IT *SOUNDS* CRAZY, BUT *YES*, I THINK SO.

YOU'RE RIGHT! *YOU ARE CRAZY!*

...EXCUSE ME?

WHAT?

THIS PERSON HASN'T SEEN ANYTHING....I MEAN C'MON, A *SCUBA TANK?* WAS HE *STARTING* THE FIRE OR *PUTTING* IT OUT?

BIL-- CAPTAIN!!!

OKAY, OKAY, WHICH WAY DID *"AQUAMAN"* GO?

UHM... DOWN THAT WAY.

C'MON, MARY, LET'S SEE IF WE CAN *SPOT* THIS GUY FROM THE AIR.

WHAT THE HECK WAS *THAT?*

OH, BROTHER! ARE WE GOING TO *START* THIS AGAIN?

LISTEN, *"BROTHER"*...IF YOU'RE EVEN *THAT* ANYMORE.

WHAT'S *THAT* SUPPOSED TO MEAN?

IT MEANS THAT THERE'S *SOMETHING* WRONG! YOU HAVEN'T CHANGED INTO BILLY FOR WHAT MUST BE AT LEAST *THREE* DAYS.

YOU'RE ACTING *NOTHING* LIKE YOURSELF AT ALL, YOU'RE BEING MEAN AND HURTFUL TO EVERYONE FOR *NO REASON* WHATSOEVER.

I DON'T SPOT ANYTHING FROM UP HERE; I GUESS OUR ELUSIVE FIRE STARTER MUST HAVE GONE *UNDERWATER*--HEH! I WONDER IF HE'S GOT SPECIAL MATCHES THAT CAN LIGHT UNDERWATER.

ARE YOU EVEN *LISTENING* TO ME?

NO...THAT'S WHY I'M GOING HOME.

SO--ANY *LUCK* WITH THIS "ARSON FIEND"?

≋*Burp*≋ NAH... APPARENTLY HE MUST BE HIDING IN HIS SECRET *UNDERWATER LAIR.*

ISN'T THAT *RIGHT,* MARY?

IT'S *OBVIOUS* THIS PERSON IS DOING THIS FOR ONE OF TWO REASONS. HE EITHER *LIKES* DOING IT OR HE'S DOING IT FOR *MONEY.*

NOW, FROM THE REPORTS I'VE SEEN ON TV, NEARLY ALL OF THE BUILDINGS THAT HAVE BEEN SET ON FIRE HAVE BEEN ABANDONED OR EMPTY.

MOST OF THEM ARE IN THE DOWNTOWN DISTRICT WHERE I USED TO SACK OUT A LOT ON COLD WINTER NIGHTS.

THE FIRES WOULDN'T REALLY *GAIN* ANYONE ANYTHING FROM BURNING THEM DOWN, UNLESS YOU HAD A *MONETARY* STAKE IN THEM.

SO?

I WOULD CONCENTRATE MY EFFORTS THERE... FIGHT FIRE WITH FIRE, SO TO SPEAK.

FIRE WITH FIRE? HA HA! THAT'S *RIDICULOUS!* YOU'RE ALMOST AS BAD AS THAT *LADY* THAT SAID THE GUY WAS WEARING A SCUBA TANK!

BILLY!

PERFECT!

FWOOOSH

YOU KNOW... YOU'VE BEEN A *HARD* GUY TO TRACK DOWN.

WHAT? AHHH.

WHAT? WHAT DO YOU WANT?

WHAT DO I WANT? ARE YOU *SERIOUS*?

PLEASE, I'M NOT *HURTING* ANYONE!

NOT HURTING ANYONE? HOW DO YOU EXPLAIN THOSE PEOPLE I HAD TO PULL OUT OF THAT *FIRE* A COUPLE OF DAYS AGO?

I...I DIDN'T KNOW...

YOU *DIDN'T* KNOW?

UGH! LISTEN TO ME, I SOUND LIKE A SKIPPING *G-POD* PLAYER.

YOU GOTTA BELIEVE ME! I DIDN'T KNOW. ALL THE BUILDINGS I SET ON FIRE WERE *SUPPOSED* TO BE ABANDONED. I WAS *PAID* BY THE OWNERS TO SET THE FIRES...

I *NEEDED* THE MONEY BUT I NEVER *MEANT* TO HURT ANYONE. I DIDN'T KNOW THERE WERE PEOPLE THERE WHEN I SET THEM ABLAZE. THEY WERE NEVER SUPPOSED TO BE THERE...

FLICK

MRRAANG

OOOPS! SORRY. **DIDN'T KNOW** YOU WERE THERE!

YOU CAN SEE HOW THAT ARGUMENT **DOESN'T** WORK, CAN'T YOU?

DON'T-- DON'T COME ANY CLOSER! I DON'T WANT TO HAVE TO USE THESE!

PLEASE... LIKE **THOSE** ARE GOING TO HURT ME.

WHAT'S HAPPENING?

I'M PUTTING AN END TO THIS.

POW

SKKRASH

WHAT ARE YOU DOING?!!!

HE DOESN'T HAVE ANY **SUPERPOWERS!** YOU HIT A NORMAL GUY THAT HARD...YOU'RE GOING TO KILL HIM!

OH MY GOSH!!! HE'S *STILL* IN THERE!! WE HAVE TO GO GET HIM!

WEEEEWOOOOWEEEEWOOOOO

LATER, AT HOME...

WHAT IS *WRONG* WITH YOU?! WHEN YOU ARE CAPTAIN MARVEL YOU ARE A *TOTAL JERK*, I WANT *BILLY* BACK!

LISTEN, *SHRIMP!* BILLY IS NOT COMING BACK... *EVER!* I'M HAVING WAY TOO MUCH *FUN* LIKE THIS!

KIDS, WHAT'S HAPPENING OUT HERE? WHAT'S ALL THE YELLING AND ARGUING ABOUT?

NOTHING! GO BACK TO YOUR *LITTER BOX*, OLD MAN!

WHEN YOU'RE BILLY YOU'RE *FINE*, BUT *NOT* WHEN YOU'RE CAPTAIN MARVEL!

LISTEN, LITTLE *GIRL*, WHY DON'T YOU MAKE YOURSELF *USEFUL* AND GET ME ANOTHER SODA?

ENOUGH OF THIS!!

I...I WANTED TO CHANGE BACK...BUT I COULDN'T.

IT'S LIKE I HAD NO CONTROL AT ALL. I COULD SEE AND HEAR AND FEEL THE THINGS I WAS DOING...BUT I WAS *HELPLESS* TO STOP IT.

ARE YOU OKAY?

I DON'T KNOW. IT WAS *WEIRD!*

IS THIS SOME SORT OF EFFECT FROM WHAT *SIVANA* DID?

I DON'T KNOW.

...WHAT DO WE DO NOW?

I DON'T KNOW... ...BUT I DO KNOW ONE THING...

...I CAN *NEVER* BE CAPTAIN MARVEL AGAIN!

BECK & PARKER APARTMENTS

A GUY **COULD** GET USED TO THIS!

I CAN LIVE ON THE STREETS... ACTUALLY HAVE FOR YEARS, BUT A GUY CAN GET USED TO A SWEET CUP OF STEAMING CHOCOLATE **ANYTIME** YOU WANT ONE TO SHAKE OFF THE CHILL IN YOUR BONES.

RECUPERATING HERE HAS BEEN A BLESSING. THE KIDS HAVE BEEN SO GOOD TO ME.

SIVANA REALLY BEAT ALL OF US UP BUT GOOD. I GUESS I GOT A LOT OF THE **PHYSICAL** BEATING UP BUT THE KIDS TOOK A LOT OF THE **EMOTIONAL STUFF.**

HE MANAGED TO FIND OUT WHERE THEY LIVE. HE STOLE THE MAGICAL LIGHTNING TO KICKSTART HIS **MECHANICAL MONSTROSITY** AND THEN USED ME AS A CONDUIT TO FUNNEL THAT ENERGY INTO IT.

SHE'S A SWEET KID.

SHE HAS TOO MUCH **HEART!** WEARS IT ON HER SLEEVE. SHE **CARES** ABOUT BILLY.

IF IT WASN'T FOR HER, BILLY WOULD BE IN A **HEAP** OF TROUBLES RIGHT NOW.

MARY IS THE ONE THAT CONVINCED CAPTAIN MARVEL TO TURN **BACK** INTO BILLY AND HELPED HIM REALIZE THERE WAS SOMETHING WRONG!

BILLY...TOSSING AND TURNING, YOU CAN TELL HE'S RESTLESS, EVEN AS HE SLEEPS.

HE'S SUCH A GOOD KID, BUT THE WEIGHT OF THE WORLD IS PRESSING DOWN ON TOP OF HIM.

IT WAS ALL LITTLE MARY AND I COULD DO TO CONVINCE HIM TO TRY AND GET SOME SLEEP BEFORE MAKING A TRIP TO THE ROCK OF ETERNITY TO SEE THE **WIZARD SHAZAM.**

I WISH I COULD GO WITH THEM, BUT WITH BILLY NOT ABLE TO TRANSFORM INTO CAPTAIN MARVEL, THE ONLY WAY TO REACH THE ROCK OF ETERNITY IS WITH THE MAGICAL PORTAL IN THE TRAIN STATION, BUT I'M IN NO SHAPE TO TRAVEL.

I HOPE THEY ARE ABLE TO GET SOME WELL DESERVED REST BEFORE THE LONG TRIP AHEAD OF THEM.

LET'S JUST HOPE IT'S AN **UNEVENTFUL** TRIP...

C'MON MARY, THE ABANDONED SUBWAY STATION IS RIGHT UP ON THE NEXT BLOCK.

I REALLY WISH TAWNY WERE ABLE TO GO WITH US. I THINK THE WIZARD MIGHT HAVE BEEN ABLE TO HELP HIM.

I THINK THE BEST THING FOR HIM IS TO REST. THE TRIP WOULD JUST TIRE HIM OUT.

GEEZ! IS EVERYONE IN THE DOWNTOWN AREA IN THIS MUCH OF A HURRY ALL THE TIME?

WELCOME TO THE BIG CITY. HOW DO YOU THINK I WAS ABLE TO LIVE ON MY OWN FOR SO LONG? ADULTS DON'T EVEN SEEM TO NOTICE WHEN YOU ARE A KID SOMETIMES.

BUMP

IS THIS WHAT IT'S LIKE ALL THE TIME WHEN YOU COME DOWN TO THE STATION? PEOPLE JUST ALL OVER THE PLACE?

YEAH... PRETTY MUCH.

OOOOF!

WHOA! I'M WALKING OVER HERE!

I DON'T CARE IF YOU SAY THAT'S NORMAL FOR THE CITY, IT'S JUST PLAIN RUDE!

WELL, *USUALLY* WHEN THEY RUN YOU OVER THEY'RE A BIT MORE *POLITE* THAN THAT.

HEY! DO YOU NOTICE SOMETHING *WEIRD?*

EVERY TIME I COME DOWN *HERE* I *NOTICE SOMETHING WEIRD.* GIANT ROBOTS, EVEN BIGGER, MORE GIANTER MONSTERS FROM ANOTHER DIMENSION...

WAIT...IS *"GIANTER"* EVEN A WORD?

NATIONAL BANK OF FAWCETT CITY

NO, I'M *SERIOUS!*

SO AM I... GIANT. GIANTER? GIANTER...ER?

LOOK AT THESE PEOPLE... THEY'RE ALL *ZONED* OUT.

YEAH, YOU'RE RIGHT! IT'S LIKE THEY'RE ALL *ZOMBIFIED!* IS THIS WHAT YOU BECOME WHEN YOU'RE AN ADULT AND THEY SAY YOU BECOME A *SLAVE* TO YOUR JOB?

WHERE ARE THEY ALL GOING?

THEY'RE ALL GOING INTO THE *BANK.*

SO WHAT? PEOPLE GO TO THE BANK ALL THE TIME! *WE* NEED TO GET TO THE SUBWAY STATION TO GET TO THE ROCK OF ETERNITY.

NO, THIS IS DIFFERENT! IT'S LIKE THEY'RE *UNDER* A SPELL OR SOMETHING... *C'MON,* WE SHOULD LOOK INTO THIS.

WE **GOTTA** GET IN THERE AND HELP THOSE PEOPLE!

WHOA! YOU'RE NOT GOING ANYWHERE! YOU **CAN'T** CHANGE INTO CAPTAIN MARVEL, REMEMBER?

HOW CAN I **FORGET** WITH YOU **REMINDING** ME EVERY COUPLE OF MINUTES?

YOU FIND A WAY TO CALL THE POLICE...I'LL CHANGE AND SEE WHAT I CAN DO.

KRAKOOM

SHAZAM!

MY G-POD!

HEY MAN, WHAT'S GOING ON?

OH, UH...I JUST SAW MARY MARVEL FLY INTO THAT BANK.

WHY? IS THERE SOMETHING GOING ON IN THERE?

LET'S MOVE IT PEOPLE, THERE'S *LOTS* OF OTHER BANKS IN THIS CITY WE NEED TO GET TO!

DUDE! WHAT ARE YOU DOING?

YOU KNOW, MY OLD MAN WAS *RIGHT,* YOU CAN'T TRUST *ANYONE* ANYMORE. I *THOUGHT* WE HAD A BRAIN CONNECTION, YOU AND ME.

UUUHH... *NO...* YOU'RE A BANK ROBBER.

DUDE...SO LIKE MY *DAD.* HE NEVER THOUGHT I WOULD AMOUNT TO MUCH EITHER, BUT I TOOK HIS *IDEA* AND BROUGHT IT UP TO DATE.

HE WAS, LIKE, *VINYL* IN A NEW AGE WORLD OF HEAVY METAL ROCK-N-ROLL *MICROCHIPS!*

WHAT ARE YOU *TALKING* ABOUT?

MR. BANJO! MY DAD!

WHO?

EXACTLY!!! HE WAS A BANJO-PLAYING *HYPNOTIST* FROM BACK IN THE DAY, BUT NO ONE EVEN *REMEMBERS* HIM! BUT TODAY, LITTLE DUDE, *EVERYONE'S* GOING TO REMEMBER ME!

EVERYONE IS GOING TO REMEMBER THE ALL OUT ROCK TALENTS OF *AXE!!*

I LIKED YOU, LITTLE DUDE. EVERY ROCK AND ROLLER NEEDS A *ROADIE,* AND I *WAS* GONNA LET YOU BE THAT ROADIE, BUT YOU JUST PROVED TO ME YOU'RE NOT *WORTHY.*

DUDE, I'M *GONNA* HAVE TO LET YOU GO!

KRAKAKOOM

I...

I DID IT!

I *FOUGHT* WHATEVER THAT IS INSIDE ME AND I *WON!*

WHEN AXE HYPNOTIZED ME AND MADE ME OVERCOME MY GREATEST FEAR--THE *THING* I FEARED MOST WAS THE FEELING OF *EVIL AND MADNESS* I EXPERIENCE WHEN I BECOME CAPTAIN MARVEL.

WHEN I CHANGED INTO CAPTAIN MARVEL IT *MUST* HAVE BROKEN THE HYPNOTIC SPELL AXE HAD CAST OVER ME, AND I WAS ABLE TO FIGHT BACK....I WAS ABLE TO *OVERCOME* MY FEAR!!!

MARY!

WE HAVE YOU **SURROUNDED**! COME OUT WITH YOUR **HANDS UP**!

OH NO!

WHOOOSH

I'M **WARNING** YOU! I AIN'T **GIVING UP**, COPS! I'LL GIVE YOU TEN MINUTES TO LEAVE OR YOU WILL ALL BE **WORKING** FOR ME WHEN I COME OUT AND PLAY MY GUITAR!

BILLY?

WHAT ARE **YOU** DOING HERE?

OH...UH... FOLLOWING A NEWS STORY. THIS BANK HAS BEEN TAKEN OVER BY SOME CRAZY ROCK-N-ROLL **WANNA**-BE NAMED AXE.

WAS THAT **MARY MARVEL** I JUST SAW THERE?

YEAH, I THINK SHE AND EVERYONE ELSE IN THE BANK HAVE BEEN **HYPNOTIZED** BY THIS PSYCHO. HE'S ABLE TO CONTROL THEM SOMEHOW WITH THE "**MUSIC**" HE PLAYS WITH HIS GUITAR.

OH MY GOSH! *CAPTAIN MARVEL* HAS BEEN HYPNOTIZED?

UH...NO, I DON'T THINK HE'S IN THERE.

REALLY? I *WONDER* WHERE HE IS? HE AND MARY MARVEL *USUALLY* WORK TOGETHER.

I'M SURE I DON'T KNOW WHERE HE IS.

HEY KID, *YOU* FEELING OK?

OH, YES, I'M FINE...IT'S JUST...

NEVER MIND...IT'S NOTHING.

C'MON KID, SPIT IT OUT. *REPORTERS* LIKE US DON'T HAVE THE *LUXURY* OF PUTTING THINGS OFF WHEN WE'VE GOT A JOB TO DO. AS MR. MORRIS *LIKES* TO SAY: "THE NEWS WAITS FOR *NO MAN!*"

ALTHOUGH I'M PRETTY SURE HE CAME UP WITH THAT SAYING *BEFORE* THE TURN OF THE *LAST* CENTURY AND WOMEN WERE *ALLOWED* IN THE WORKPLACE.

WELL, SOMETIMES I FEEL LIKE I'M *NOT* STRONG ENOUGH TO DO WHAT *NEEDS* TO BE DONE.

WELL KID, IN THE NEWS BIZ, YOU SEE A LOT OF STUFF, BUT ONE THING I DO KNOW IS THAT YOU ARE A *TOUGH* LITTLE KID.

ATIONAL B
OF *FAWCETT CITY*

I'M *SERIOUS.* LOOK AT THE THINGS YOU HAVE BEEN ABLE TO ACCOMPLISH SO FAR, AND AT *YOUR AGE,* DON'T LET *ANYONE* EVER TELL YOU THAT YOU *CAN'T* DO SOMETHING. YOU PUT YOUR MIND TO IT, YOU CAN DO *ANYTHING.*

YOU *REALLY* THINK SO?

ABSOLUTELY, KID. YOU ARE SMART, FUNNY AND NOT TO MENTION *CUTE* AS THE DICKENS, AND YOU ALWAYS REMEMBER MY CUP OF COFFEE AND *THAT* GOES A LONG WAY IN MY BOOK. SO DON'T EVER SELL YOURSELF SHORT.

GARY, LET'S GET A SHOT OF THE BANK AND SEE IF WE CAN GET SET UP TO GET A SHOT OF CAPTAIN MARVEL WHEN HE SHOWS UP, TOO!

NOT TO WORRY KID, *CAPTAIN MARVEL* WILL PROBABLY SHOW UP ANY MINUTE AND SAVE THE DAY.

I DON'T THINK SO...

...BUT I KNOW THAT I'M STILL *CAPABLE* OF DOING SOMETHING.

WHAT ARE WE SUPPOSED TO DO NOW?

SHOULD WE GET MORE GUNS?

WHERE'S CAPTAIN MARVEL?

THEY DON'T EVEN SEE ME...

THAT'S IT! THAT'S WHY HE DOESN'T WANT ANY COINS...OR ANY *OTHER METAL* NEAR HIM...OR MORE SPECIFICALLY HIS GUITAR!

HEY, DID THAT LITTLE *SCARLET GIRL* BLOW UP?

I THINK YOU HAVE *OTHER* THINGS TO WORRY ABOUT, AXE!

WHOA, LITTLE DUDE! WHERE DID YOU COME FROM?

OUCH!

TCHING

CLANG

CLING

DUDE, YOU LIKE, GOT ANY ASPIRIN? I GOT A *KILLER* HEADACHE.

THANKS FOR SAVING ME BACK THERE.

NATIONAL BANK OF FAWCETT CITY

I THINK IT WAS *SMART* TO GET OUT OF THERE BEFORE ANYONE *REALIZED* EITHER ONE OF US WERE THERE.

YEAH, WELL, IT SEEMS LIKE I HAVE TO DO *ALL* THE THINKING AROUND HERE LATELY!

THAT IS NOT TRUE!

... I'M SURE I WOULD HAVE BROKEN FREE... EVENTUALLY.

OH PLEASE, YOU ARE SO *USELESS.*

IT'S NOT JUST *THAT*, THERE'S SOMETHING **WRONG** WITH ME TOO. WHEN I SMASHED AXE IN THE HEAD WITH THE GUITAR...I **ENJOYED** IT.

WELL, HE DESERVED IT! HE WAS A *JERK!*

NO.

I *REALLY* ENJOYED IT. I WANTED TO DO IT *AGAIN*...A COUPLE OF TIMES. IT TOOK **ALL** MY WILL POWER TO PUT DOWN THE GUITAR AND NOT HIT THAT GUY AGAIN *EVEN* WHEN HE WAS OUT COLD.

WHAT ARE YOU SAYING, BILLY?

I THINK THAT WHATEVER IT IS THAT MAKES CAPTAIN MARVEL MEAN AND EVIL, IS *STARTING* TO AFFECT ME TOO. I CAN FEEL MYSELF *SLIPPING* AWAY AS IF SOMETHING IS TAKING OVER AND IF WE DON'T GET TO THE WIZARD SOON...

...IT MIGHT BE *TOO* LATE.

THE LEGACY OF MR. BANJO!

WRITERS: ART BALTAZAR & FRANCO   ARTIST: BYRON VAUGHNS
COLORS: DAVID TANGUAY   LETTERS: TRAVIS LANHAM   COVER: BYRON VAUGHNS
ASST. EDITOR: SIMONA MARTORE   EDITOR: DAN DIDIO

I CAN'T HELP BUT THINK OF THE WORD. THE WIZARD'S NAME.

Solomon
Hercules
Atlas
Zeus
Achilles
Mercury

THAT WORD MEANS A LOT.

YOU TEND TO TAKE IT FOR GRANTED.

I KNOW IT'S THE WIZARD'S NAME, BUT WHEN YOU THINK OF THE NAMES THAT MAKE IT UP...

I MEAN...WOW! THERE ARE SOME HEAVY DUTY POWER HITTERS IN THERE.

THAT IS EXACTLY WHY I'M AFRAID TO SAY THE WORD! FOR FEAR THAT I'LL TURN INTO CAPTAIN MARVEL. IT'S TAKING ALL MY STRENGTH TO FIGHT WHATEVER IT IS THAT'S TRYING TO TAKE ME OVER!

THAT'S WHY WE'VE COME HERE TO SEE...

SORRY TO INTERRUPT SIR, BUT BILLY *REALLY* NEEDS YOUR HELP!

MY WORD, BILLY. WHAT HAS HAPPENED?

WE DON'T KNOW EXACTLY, ALL WE KNOW IS FIRST CAPTAIN MARVEL WAS TURNING ALL *MEAN* AND *EVIL* AND NOW THE *SAME THING* IS HAPPENING TO BILLY!

...

BILLY?

PLEASE SIR, HE'S JUST *BARELY* HOLDING IT TOGETHER! YOU *NEED* TO HELP HIM!

IT'S... DIFFICULT...TO CONCENTRATE...

THIS IS *MOST* DISTRESSING.

NO.

YOU KNOW WHAT IT IS? WHAT'S *DOING* THIS TO HIM?

THE *MOST* DISTRESSING THING ABOUT THIS IS THAT I DID NOT FORESEE IT! THERE IS *SOMETHING* WRONG WITH HIM AND WE MUST DRAW IT OUT.

THAT'S GREAT, *RIGHT?* YOU CAN DO THAT?

MOST LIKELY. THE PROBLEM IS THAT IF WE DO DRAW *WHATEVER* IT IS OUT, THERE IS NO TELLING WHAT IT COULD BE.

BILLY, YOU MUST CHANGE INTO CAPTAIN MARVEL.

WHAT!!? IS YOUR SKULL FULL OF *WET NOODLES* OR SOMETHING?

MARY!

NO, TAWNY, IT'S ALL RIGHT.

THIS MAY BE ETERNITY, BUT IF HE CHANGES INTO CAPTAIN MARVEL, WE'RE NEVER GOING TO SEE IT AGAIN...*EVER!*

THAT'S ENOUGH, MARY.

I SENSE THIS *"EVIL"* THAT YOU TALK ABOUT WITHIN BILLY, BUT *MORE* WITHIN CAPTAIN MARVEL. IT IS THE LATTER WE WILL NEED HERE IF WE ARE TO DRAW OUT THE TRUTH BEHIND ALL OF THIS.

WELL, IF YOU SAY SO, BUT I CAN'T SEE *ANYTHING* GOOD COMING OUT OF THIS.

I KNOW YOU ARE WORRIED ABOUT HIM; IT IS AN *ADMIRABLE* TRAIT FOR A SISTER.

WE ARE WORRIED FOR HIM AS WELL, BUT FEAR NOT, DEAR CHILD, SOME OF US HAVE HAD EXPERIENCE WITH THE WORKINGS OF *MAGIC* BEFORE.

YOU THINK *THIS* HAS SOMETHING TO DO WITH MAGIC?

IT HAS ALL THE TRAPPINGS, BUT WE SHALL FIND OUT SOON ENOUGH.

BILLY, YOU MUST TRANSFORM INTO CAPTAIN MARVEL IF WE ARE TO **SOLVE** THIS MYSTERY.

BUT...YOU TOLD ME...TO NEVER SAY THE...WORD HERE...THAT MAGIC IS... UNPREDICTABLE.

YES, YOUNG ONE, YOU ARE **CORRECT.** THE RULES OF THE ORDINARY WORLD DO NOT APPLY HERE IN ETERNITY, BUT I FEAR IN YOUR **CONDITION** WE MAY HAVE NO OTHER CHOICE.

YOU MAY SIMPLY NOT SURVIVE IF WE DO NOT PROCEED QUICKLY.

WELL... IF YOU SAY SO...

I KNOW IT WILL BE DIFFICULT, BUT ONCE YOU TRANSFORM, TRY TO STAY IN CONTROL AS MUCH AS POSSIBLE.

HE CAN DO IT! HE HAS HIS **FAMILY** HERE TO HELP HIM!

SHAZAM...

MASTER! YOU...NEED TO...HURRY... I'M LOSING CONTROL!

ARE YOU OKAY? HOW DO YOU FEEL?

ACTUALLY... *BETTER*.

NOT ONLY BETTER--I FEEL *GREAT!* LIKE ALL OF THAT EVIL STUFF IS GONE!

LIKE, *TOTALLY* GONE? WHERE DID IT GO?

THERE.

YLLANIF I MA EERF!

DID HE JUST SAY SOMETHING? WHAT DID HE SAY?

I DON'T KNOW, BUT HE LOOKS *JUST* LIKE YOU! FREAKY!

THIS IS OBVIOUSLY THE PHYSICAL MANIFESTATION OF ALL OF YOUR BOTTLED UP "EVIL."

HE'S THE SPITTING IMAGE OF CAPTAIN MARVEL!

I WAS ABLE TO DRAW OUT ALL OF THE MADNESS AND DEVIANCE I COULD FIND WITHIN YOUR PSYCHE AND CONTAIN IT WITHIN A PHYSICAL PARAMETER...

CURIOUS THAT IT HAS TAKEN THE FORM OF CAPTAIN MARVEL.

IS THAT ALL OF HIS EVIL?

IS IT GOING TO HURT US?

NO, THAT WOULD NOT--

I LLIW YORTSED UOY!

OOOOFF!

SLAM

WHAT WAS THAT!???

I DON'T KNOW.

EVIL.

RIGHT BEFORE IT ATTACKED, I SENSED A *RAGE* LIKE NONE OTHER AND...*EVIL.*

WHAT? I THOUGHT YOU SAID IT *WOULDN'T* HURT US!

AS I HAVE STATED BEFORE, USING MAGIC HERE AT THE POINT OF ETERNITY CAN CAUSE A *PARADOX*--

WELL, DUH!

WHAM

WE *NEED* TO HELP HIM!

I'M ON-- OOOOW!

SWAT

WHY IS TAWNY...LIKE *THAT?*

MAGIC IS VERY *UNPREDICTABLE* HERE. IT SEEMS THAT CAPTAIN MARVEL'S DOPPLEGANGER--

YOU MEAN HIS *EVIL TWIN!*

CAPTAIN MARVEL IS A BEING OF MAGIC, SO IT STANDS TO REASON THAT HIS..."EVIL TWIN" IS MADE FROM THE *SAME* MAGIC.

WHEN HE STRUCK TAWNY, IT SEEMS HE MAY HAVE STOPPED HIM FROM *COMPLETELY* TRANSFORMING.

YOU MEAN HE COULD BE *STUCK* LIKE THIS FOREVER?

I DON'T KNOW, BUT I FEAR THAT MAY BE THE *LEAST* OF OUR PROBLEMS.

WHY DO YOU SAY--

OH MY GOSH! *THAT* CAN'T BE GOOD!

NO, IT IS NOT! I THOUGHT THERE WAS A FAMILIAR FEELING TO ALL OF THIS.

BILLY IS *NOT* FIGHTING AN EVIL VERSION OF HIMSELF...HE'S FIGHTING SOMETHING MUCH, MUCH *WORSE!*

I THINK I'VE FIGURED IT OUT! YOU'RE A *MIRROR IMAGE* OF ME, RIGHT DOWN TO THE *SPEECH PATTERN!* YOU'RE TALKING BACKWARDS!

YLTNERAPPA UOY ERA TCERROC, LL'I ETASNEPMOC ROF TAHT NI EMIT... LITNU NEHT--

UOY LLIW EB ENOG!

I'M *TRYING* TO HELP YOU BUT I'M ALSO NOT GOING TO LET YOU HURT ME!

UOY NAC YRT, TUB I LLIW TRUH UOY!

KERSMASH

DOWN!

THUD

THANKS, MARY. HE'S ANGRY AND PRETTY CONFUSED. WE NEED TO TRY AND *HELP* HIM.

NO... HE'S *NOT!* YOU NEED... TO *STOP* HIM!

I'M TRYING TO COMMUNICATE WITH HIM. I'VE FIGURED OUT HIS SPEECH PATTERN, BUT--

NO! WE NEED TO TAKE HIM OUT *NOW!* FAST!

I'VE HAD A STRING OF LUCK LATELY! YOU MAY QUESTION IF IT'S **GOOD** LUCK OR **BAD** LUCK...WELL, THAT **DEPENDS** ON YOUR POINT OF VIEW...

BLACK ADAM WAS THE WIZARD'S **FIRST** CHOICE AS A CHAMPION HERE ON EARTH MANY YEARS AGO, BUT IT DIDN'T **WORK OUT** SO WELL.

SOLOMON--WISDOM

DR. SIVANA HAS BEEN NOTHING BUT A **PAIN.** HE'S TRIED DOING EVERYTHING HE CAN TO STOP US, INCLUDING THROWING A **GIANT ROBOT** AT US, NOT ONCE, BUT **TWICE.**

HERCULES--STRENGTH

APPARENTLY, WHEN SIVANA TORE UP THE CITY WITH HIS GIANT ROBOT MR. ATOM, HE **AWAKENED** A LONG DORMANT PSYCHO FROM LONG AGO THAT **STILL** WANTS TO RULE THE WORLD.

ATLAS--STAMINA

AND THEN THERE'S THE LOCAL CRAZIES, LIKE THE **ARSON FIEND.** HE WAS SETTING FIRES ALL OVER FAWCETT CITY, ENDANGERING **HUNDREDS** OF LIVES...

ZEUS--POWER

...OR THE HYPNOTIZING AXE, THAT WAS TRYING TO LIVE UP TO HIS DAD'S NAME BY ROBBING BANKS.

ACHILLES--COURAGE

TO TOP IT ALL OFF, I RECENTLY FOUGHT A MIRROR IMAGE OF **MYSELF** FULL OF NASTY EVILNESS THAT TURNED OUT TO BE **MR. MIND!**

SOME MAY THINK THAT'S BEEN A STRING OF **BAD** LUCK! I THINK GETTING TO BE CAPTAIN MARVEL IS THE **COOLEST** THING THAT COULD **EVER** HAPPEN TO A KID!

IF YOU'RE THINKING BAD LUCK, JUST FACTOR IN THAT I **BEAT** ALL OF THOSE GUYS!

MERCURY--SPEED

UOY ERA A LO-... YOU ARE A *FOOL!!*

WHAT? WHY DID I CHANGE?

APPARENTLY, THERE ARE *MANY* THINGS TO BE LEARNED...

I HAVE BEEN LYING *DORMANT* IN YOUR HEAD SINCE OUR *LAST* ENCOUNTER.

OW.

IT TOOK ME A BIT OF TIME BUT I WAS *STARTING* TO TAKE CONTROL OF YOU IN THERE...HAD YOU *WORRIED* FOR A WHILE, DIDN'T I?

BUT *JUST* AS PREDICTED, *YOU* SET ME FREE.

THANK YOU...NOW SAY *GOODBYE* TO HUMANITY.

SHAZAM!

OH, DON'T LOOK SO SURPRISED! *YOU'RE* THE ONE THAT *CHANGED* THE RULES!

YOU WERE THE ONE TO COME TO US. *YOU* RIPPED A BIG GIANT HOLE IN TIME AND SPACE, ALLOWING MYSELF AND THE REST OF MY *MONSTER SOCIETY* INTO *YOUR* DIMENSION.

DO YOU EXPECT THINGS TO WORK *EXACTLY* THE SAME IN BOTH DIMENSIONS? HOW *LIMITED* IN BRAIN CAPACITY YOU HUMANS ARE!

YOU BROUGHT US HERE...

SHAZAM! SHAZAM! SHAZAM!

...AND WHEN *YOU* DID THAT, YOU SIGNED THIS PLANET'S *EXPIRATION DATE.*

HANDS OFF, YOU SLIMY, LITTLE WORM!

ARRRRGH!!!!

TRY TO *LAY* STILL, MY OLD FRIEND.

WHAT...WHAT HAPPENED?

IT WAS THE VILLAINOUS MR. MIND.

HOW?

APPARENTLY, MR. MIND HAS BEEN HIDING *DORMANT* INSIDE YOUNG BILLY'S PSYCHE...

WHEN CAPTAIN MARVEL *DEFEATED* MR. MIND WITH THAT PUNCH THAT *RIPPED* OPEN TIME AND SPACE, THEY WERE BOTH PULLED BACK TO ETERNITY.

WHEN MARY HELPED BILLY TURN BACK INTO CAPTAIN MARVEL AFTER THAT, MR. MIND *MUST* HAVE COME BACK WITHIN HIS *SUBCONSCIOUS* AND WAS JUST BIDING HIS TIME TO EXACT HIS REVENGE.

I NEED TO...TRY AND HELP...

YOU ARE IN A GREAT DEAL OF PAIN.

I SEEM TO BE *STUCK* IN MID... TRANSFORMATION! I CAN FEEL...MY BODY... EITHER *WANTING* TO BE A MAN OR...A TIGER... BUT I *CAN'T* CHANGE INTO EITHER!

I DON'T KNOW IF THERE IS *ANYTHING* I CAN DO. GETTING STRUCK WITH THE RESIDUAL EFFECTS FROM *NIATPAC LEVRAM'S* LIGHTNING HERE AT THE POINT OF *ETERNITY*, HAS HAD AN *ADVERSE* EFFECT ON YOUR PHYSIOLOGY.

I FEAR YOU MAY *NOT* BE ABLE TO *TRANSFORM* AT ALL ANYMORE...

YOU MAY BE *STUCK* IN THIS FORM FOREVER!

MAZAHS!

KRAKOOM

YES!

HOW DOES *THAT* WORK? YOU COULDN'T CHANGE A SECOND AGO!

I THINK I'M *BACK* ON TRACK AGAIN. THINGS ARE MESSED UP BECAUSE HE'S MY *OPPOSITE*--

WHEN WE CHANGED, HE USED HIS MAGIC WORD, WHICH AFFECTED *BOTH* OF US BECAUSE WE'RE *BOTH* MAGICAL BEINGS. I THINK I GOT IT NOW.

NOW, LET'S GO SHUT THIS *WORM* DOWN!

YOU SWOOP *AROUND* AND TAKE HIM OUT AT THE KNEES...

I'M GOING TO *PUNCH* HIM RIGHT IN THE FACE!

...WHAT IS *THAT* EXPRESSION THEY USE ON THIS WORLD? "LIKE A MOTH TO A FLAME."

WHAT THE--?

OOOOOF!

MONSTERS!

WHERE DID *THESE* GUYS COME FROM?

I CALLED THEM.

YOU'VE BEEN STUCK IN MY HEAD UNTIL A FEW MINUTES AGO! HOW DID YOU DO THAT?

I MADE A **DEVICE** TO CONTACT MY MONSTERS STRANDED HERE FROM OUR **LAST ENCOUNTER.**

I WAS ABLE TO CREATE A **SIGNALING** DEVICE WHEN YOU WERE **ASLEEP.** IT TOOK ME **WEEKS** WITH THE LIMITED SUPPLIES FROM AROUND YOUR APARTMENT.

IT WASN'T EASY WITH THE EVEN MORE LIMITED TECHNOLOGY OF THIS WORLD. I COULD ONLY WORK A FEW HOURS EACH NIGHT, AS YOU WOULD **ALWAYS** RESIST ME AND **WAKE UP.**

THAT EXPLAINS **WHY** I WAS SO **TIRED** ALL THE TIME!

AND HAVING WORM FREAK **INSIDE** YOUR HEAD, EXPLAINS WHY YOU WERE SUCH A **JERK** ALL THE TIME!

YOU HAVE NO NEED TO WORRY ABOUT **ANYTHING** ANY LONGER.

BECAUSE SOON...YOU WILL NO **LONGER** EXIST!

WHOOOSH

SLAM

SHHRIPP

OH, NO!

RUMMMMMMBLE

YOU NEED TO GO FASTER!

I'M *TRYING*, BUT NO MATTER WHAT, YOU KEEP GOING.

RUMMMMMMBLE

RUMMMMMMBLE

I'M NOT GOING TO MAKE IT! THERE MUST BE ANOTHER WAY OUT OF THIS!

HOW DO I--*WAIT!* THE WISDOM OF SOLOM--

GOOD RIDDANCE!

NOW, GET THE BRAT!

YOU THINK I'M AFRAID OF *YOU*? I'LL GET YOU BACK FOR WHAT YOU DID TO CAPTAIN MARVEL!

YOU WON'T BE ALONE!

ROAAARR!!

A LITTLE TOO LATE I'M AFRAID.

MMMMMM

WHAT THE?

MMMMMM

IMPOSSIBLE! HE'S COMING RIGHT *THROUGH* SOLID ROCK!

MMMMMM

H-HOW DID YOU PHASE THROUGH *SOLID* ROCK?

USING THE WISDOM OF SOLOMON! I WAS ABLE TO CALCULATE THE *TIMING* OF THE ELECTRONS AND ATOMS IN SOLID MATTER SO THAT I WOULD *PASS* BETWEEN THOSE IN THE RUBBLE!

BET THAT'S SOMETHING EVEN *YOU* CAN'T DO IN A COPY OF *MY BODY,* MR. MIND!

YOU'D BE *SURPRISED* WHAT I COULD *LEARN* TO DO WITH THIS BODY!

I *KNEW* YOU WOULDN'T BE ABLE TO RESIST TRYING *THAT* LITTLE TRICK!

WHAT'S THAT? I CAN'T *HEAR* YOU! HOW DID I DO THIS?

AS I TOLD YOU BEFORE, I WAS ABLE TO CALCULATE THE TIMING OF THE ELECTRONS AND ATOMS TO PASS *THROUGH* SOLID MATTER.

WHAT I DIDN'T TELL YOU WAS, A *SLIGHT* AMOUNT OF YOUR SUBSTANCE OR ESSENCE WOULD BE LEFT BEHIND *EACH* TIME YOU UTILIZED THIS FORMULA.

YOU CAN PASS THROUGH SOLID OBJECTS ONCE, OR *MAYBE* EVEN TWICE, BUT ONE THING IS *CERTAIN*, YOU CAN NEVER PASS THROUGH A REFLECTIVE *OBJECT* LIKE A *MIRROR!*

IF YOU *TRY* TO PASS THROUGH THIS TO GET OUT, TOO MUCH OF YOUR ESSENCE WOULD BE *TRAPPED*, AND YOU WOULD CEASE TO EXIST...SO YOU'RE STUCK IN THERE *FOREVER*.

TAWNY! HOW ARE--

I'LL BE FINE! I MAY *LOOK* LIKE HALF HUMAN AND HALF TIGER, BUT AS LONG AS THAT MR. MIND IS STOPPED, I CAN MAKE IT!

WHERE DID ALL OF MIND'S MONSTERS GO?

AS SOON AS THEY SAW YOU TRAPPED MIND IN THAT BIG GIANT MIRROR, THEY JUST *TOOK OFF*. I WOULD HAVE GONE AFTER THEM, BUT I DIDN'T WANT TO LEAVE TAWNY ALONE.

YOU DID THE *RIGHT* THING!

WE HAVE A *LOT* OF CLEANING UP TO DO, BUT FIRST I THINK WE SHOULD GET TAWNY *HOME*.

I DON'T THINK THAT'S SUCH A GOOD IDEA. IT WAS ONE THING WHEN I WAS IN *HUMAN* FORM, BUT NOW THAT I'M STUCK LIKE *THIS*...I JUST DON'T WANT TO BE A BURDEN!

MR. MIND OVER MATTER!

WRITTEN BY: ART BALTAZAR & FRANCO   ART BY: BYRON VAUGHNS
COLORS: DAVID TANGUAY   LETTERS: TRAVIS LANHAM   COVER: BYRON VAUGHNS
ASST. EDITOR: SIMONA MARTORE   EDITOR: DAN DIDIO

BILLY BATSON AND THE MAGIC OF SHAZAM! #1 variant cover by MIKE KUNKEL